Drawing on the Macintosh®

A Non-Artist's Guide to MacDraw,® Illustrator,® FreeHand,™ and Many Others

Drawing on the Macintosh®

A Non-Artist's Guide to MacDraw,® Illustrator,® FreeHand,™ and Many Others

Deke McClelland
Publishing Resources Incorporated

BUSINESS ONE IRWIN
Desktop Publishing Library

Homewood, IL 60430

Senior editor: Susan Glinert Stevens, Ph.D.
Production manager: Ann Cassady
Printer: R. R. Donnelley & Sons Company

Library of Congress Cataloging-in-Publication Data

McClelland, Deke, 1962–
    Drawing on the Macintosh : a non-artist's guide to MacDraw, Illustrator, FreeHand, and many others / Deke McClelland.
        p.   cm.
    Includes index.
    ISBN 1–55623–415–5
    1. Computer graphics. 2. Macintosh (Computer) I. Title.
T385.M37778   1991
006.6′76—dc20   90–38275

Printed in the United States of America

2 3 4 5 6 7 8 9 0 DO 7 6 5 4 3 2 1 0

Acknowledgements

Putting one person's name on a book cover is a little like congratulating Dad for raising such fine children, but leaving out Mom. The following people are the mothers of *Drawing on the Macintosh*:

Thanks to Bill Gladstone, Susan Glinert, and Craig Danuloff, without whose help I'd be out of Macs and into McDonalds.

Immense gratitude to Kathi Townes for going above and beyond the call of editing by helping to consolidate a final month's worth of work into a week of sleepless nights. Italia, how she beckons!

Thanks also to Juan Thompson for those interesting blend sessions, to Tom *Midgley* for eliminating my typesetting worries, to Ann Cassady for some fine work on past halftones, and to John Duane just 'cause he's such a pal.

R.D., S.R., J.G., A.E., and J.M.—who let these guys in?

Never was there such a one as EP, who can't remember the last time she was mentioned in a book. She didn't help with a word, but if I could include only one name in this list, it would be hers.

Contents

Chapter 3: The Drawing Environment 85

Part Two
Applying Your Knowledge

Part Three
Enhancing Existing Artwork

Part Four
Software Review

Appendices

Foreword

It is often said that our world is becoming more and more the domain of the specialist. As each category of human interest and endeavor becomes increasingly complex and competitive, practitioners are left with little choice but to forgo a wide range of expertise in order to develop and maintain their chosen specialization. Time does not allow, or so the theory goes, one person to be an accountant and a politician and a researcher and an artist.

On the other hand, think of all that you can do with the aid of your personal computer and some software. If you have a spell-checking program, you can spell; if you have an accounting package, you can correctly perform double-entry bookkeeping; if you have a telecommunications program, you can communicate with millions of people or search vast databases; and if you have page composition software, you can electronically "paste-up" complex documents. The personal computer may well be the anecdote to specialization.

In each of these cases, a complex process has been simplified to little more than data entry and button pushing. The tools required to perform these tasks have been computerized and the use of these tools has been automated.

However, the process of drawing has yet to—and some would argue never will—undergo such a complete transformation. While the tools of drawing have been simulated on a computer screen, the use of these tools has not been fully automated. This represents a fundamental difference between drawing and most other computerized processes: Drawing still requires that a person know how to use the tools of the trade and, more importantly, how to think like an artist.

But how many of us are equipped with this knowledge? Certainly not the average computer user—or so you may believe. Millions of people own drawing software but few dare to draw more than a map to their house. They assume that the ability to draw is solely dependent on talent, or that it requires extensive study and practice.

Drawing on the Macintosh is for those people.

In this book, Mr. McClelland demystifies the artistic process, demonstrating that by learning a few basic principles, understanding the power of your automated drawing tools, and remembering where the "Undo" command is located, almost anyone can create the kind of art they need to spruce up newsletters, reports, letters, brochures, and so on. With a little practice, you will be creating original art as easily as you already correct your spelling, balance your books, or layout the monthly newsletter. In no time you will be personalizing your work, making it more attractive, saving both time and money, and having a little more fun with your computer.

A few words of advice before you set off to become the complete Renaissance Man or Woman: Start simple, stick with it, and refer back to the elementary sections of this book often. And never be embarrassed by your early work. Just claim that it's some horrible clip-art you're trying to fix.

Best of luck.

Craig Danuloff
President, Publishing Resources Inc.

Developing a Successful Drawing Technique

CHAPTER 1

The Graphic Process

An effective graphic is an amazing thing. To the untrained eye, a graphic may be as mysterious as it is pleasing, seemingly outside the realm of personal achievement. But like a piece of furniture or a loaf of bread, an illustration is a basic work of craftsmanship. In this chapter, we'll disassemble the craft of drawing into its two basic elements of process and technique. By examining how an artist works and what an artist knows, we will gain a clearer understanding of how to create a successful graphic.

Who can draw?

A common misconception among "non-artists" is that drawing is a talent that is not so much learned as inherited at birth. In fact, most people can learn to draw passably—some even quite well—in a short period of time.

Developing an ability to draw is not the impossible task that you may believe it to be. After all, a successful graphic is measured foremost by its ability to effectively communicate an idea. As a child, you probably created a successful drawing in the form of a dot-to-dot puzzle. Even a person endowed with little more than rudimentary eye-hand coordination can move a pencil in a fairly straight line from point A to point B, from point B to point C, from point C to point D, and so on. The finished dot-to-dot image will look the same and will communicate an idea with the same clarity whether completed by a modern-day Leonardo da Vinci or a careful child. Both Leonardo and the child possess the same innate ability to connect dots with a pencil. If both also possess the same determination to accurately follow the puzzle directions, both can master this simple drawing process.

The primary difference between the experienced artist Leonardo and the inexperienced child is that the artist knows how to draw without numbered dots as a guideline. Based on experience, the artist knows:

1. where to begin and end pencil strokes to accurately represent an image;

2. which stroke to create first and which to create last;

3. what tools are available and how to operate each tool;

4. that drawing is not an exact science, and allows a generous margin for trial and error. Any stroke applied may be erased, reapplied, re-erased, and so on, until the stroke satisfies the artist's imagined design.

An artist's knowledge, like all knowledge, is gained through a combination of reading, observation, and personal experience. An artist is no more born with artistic knowledge than a banker is born with a knowledge of monetary exchange or thirty-year mortgage rates. An artist is born with the interest and attitude necessary to develop his or her drawing ability.

An artist's knowledge is gained through a combination of reading, observation, and personal experience.

The next section examines how an artist uses a personal computer to create a graphic.

The electronic graphic process

The process of creating a graphic on a computer includes four fundamental steps:

1. Determine your purpose in creating the graphic, and develop a basic concept for the graphic.

2. Create a series of rough sketches, representing every idea that you and your associates have come up with.

3. After selecting a favorite sketch, polish the sketch into a final draft or finished drawing.

4. Save the final draft and all preliminary sketches for future use.

The electronic
graphic process
is cyclic; a single
drawing can
be used over
and over.

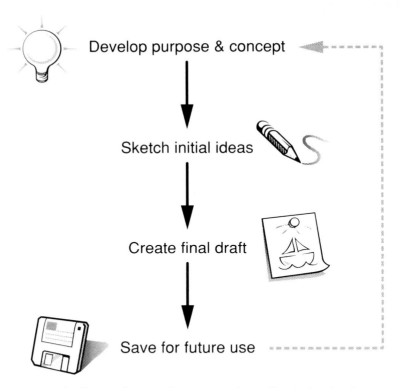

Develop purpose & concept

Sketch initial ideas

Create final draft

Save for future use

As we shall see, the graphic process is cyclic. A single electronic drawing can be used over and over again in a variety of circumstances. The icons shown in this figure appear throughout our text, highlighting discussions of corresponding topics.

The next few pages describe these four steps in the electronic graphic process in detail, and examine how each relates to other steps and to the process as a whole.

Developing purpose and concept

Before you create a single line inside any drawing program, you must have a clear idea of what you want to draw, and why. A drawing must have a definite purpose, whether it relates to a paragraph of text in a newsletter or stands alone as an illustration.

The intention of a drawing should be forthright and obvious. A successful graphic explains itself without words. A graphic should provide a viewer with enough visual information to make any surrounding text largely repetitive and should prepare the viewer for your textual message, whether commercial or personal. Outside a museum or art class environment, viewers are rarely prepared for obscure or ambiguous visual themes, making it risky to employ obscure themes in commercial artwork.

A graphic should provide viewers with enough visual information to render any surrounding text largely repetitive.

A drawing of a mortar board with a scroll requires no text to convey the theme of a high school or college graduation. It prepares the viewer to read text about graduation topics, such as party or gift information or job possibilities.

Placing our mortar board on a car roof obscures our message. Not only are mortar boards and cars unusual visual partners, but their size relationship is unrealistic. The graphic is more interesting than its predecessor, but more difficult to interpret.

A drawing's concept should be not only interesting, but should also have a clear purpose.

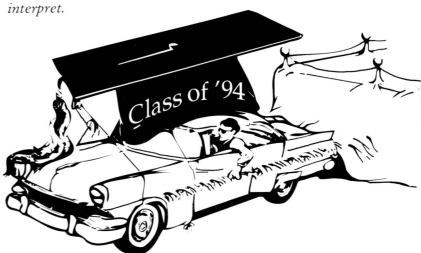

An ambiguous graphic can often be clarified by adding detail. In this case, we have transformed the surrealistic cap on a car into part of a parade float. In doing so, we have retained the graphic appeal of the previous figure while also refining its purpose.

When determining the concept for a prospective drawing, you must isolate your needs and your restrictions. Before your graphic can serve a purpose, you have to identify that purpose. Sometimes it can be helpful to make a list of your intentions. For example, if you are creating an advertisement for a brand of dog food, you know that first and foremost you want to interest dog owners. In fact, your graphic should be able to attract all dog owners. Suppose that you are also concerned that you don't offend owners of cats or birds, since your company produces many varieties of pet food. Therefore, although a drawing of a fierce retriever chasing after the neighbors' Siamese cat might amuse and attract many dog owners, it will no doubt repel cat owners and thus prove itself an unsuitable theme. You must find a happy medium that encourages dog owners to buy your brand while demonstrating to non-dog owners that your company is sympathetic to all animals.

Below are some of the most common categories of graphic needs and restrictions. Each consideration should be addressed when developing any business graphic:

To create a drawing that conveys a purpose, you must first isolate your needs and your restrictions.

Needs:

1. Primary purpose of graphic

2. General interests of the company

3. Clarity of concept

4. Overall appearance of final draft

Restrictions:

1. Time constraints, including deadlines

2. Budget constraints

3. Printing restrictions and costs

Sketching initial ideas

Once you have firmly established your intentions, you may start drawing. However, do not feel compelled to create a perfect piece of artwork on your first try. Drawing is a process, not a goal. While you draw, you will often discover ideas and possibilities that you had not considered initially. One line or shape may suggest several others, each of which may take your drawing in a different direction. By creating several sketches for a single graphic, you take advantage of many ideas, possibly more than one at a time.

Sketching in a painting program is a method for trapping ideas.

Suppose that these four sketches are a random sampling of those that we have created for the dog food advertisement. Don't worry if your sketches do not look this nice. Sketches should contain only a bare minimum of visual information to remind you of an idea later.

Sketching is a method for trapping ideas. Before you judge an idea to be good or bad, get it down on paper or on disk. The sketching process is not generally a time for evaluation; it is a time for fast, informal, and unstifled production. You will have plenty of time to scrutinize your ideas later.

Since the only purpose of a sketch is to help you organize and promote your ideas, you rarely need to worry about the quality of your artwork at this stage in the graphic process. In fact, you will probably want to create most of your sketches in a *painting* program, such as MacPaint. Unlike a drawing program, in which you define images using lines, shapes, and other smooth objects, paint programs provide simple tools—like pencils and paintbrushes—that are used to color individual dots, called *pixels*, on your computer screen. Because these tools work much like their real-world counterparts, they are ideal for sketching images.

If you are creating sketches to present to other people or to business associates for consideration, we advise you to create a second series of sketches, representing only your four or five best ideas. Polish them enough to display your skills and to effectively demonstrate your ideas.

When sketching, concentrate on organizing your ideas; don't obsess about quality.

Creating a final draft

When you begin to create a final draft, assembling a wide variety of sketches provides you with flexibility in approaching a graphic. No part of the effort required to create the final drawing need be directed toward identifying the concept. Once you have selected a favorite sketch, you may import it into a drawing program and work it into a final draft. If more than one sketch is impressive enough to warrant further deliberation, you may create final drafts for two or more sketches.

The final draft stage is your opportunity to experiment with your graphic style.

This graphic of a dog waiting patiently to be fed is not only endearing to dog owners, but also inoffensive to other pet owners. We have developed it from our first sketch in the previous figure, using a simple approach. The three objects— the owner, the dog, and the bowl—are positioned in a basic triangular arrangement.

The final draft stage is your opportunity to work in your personal drawing style, which we will discuss more fully at the end of this chapter. You may also refine your idea to more accurately fulfill your purpose.

If you're wondering how to create a final drawing, take a look at Chapters 5, 6, and 7 of this book. These chapters present the step-by-step evolution of several final drafts in an easy-to-follow fashion.

Saving drawings for future reuse

No drawing should ever be considered a waste of time. An idea turned down today may be picked up tomorrow. Save all your drawings, especially sketches. Sketches can provide a substantial resource for future works. You might be surprised to learn that many "new" graphics are really developed from sketches that were passed over several months or years ago.

Every artist keeps piles of early artwork. Although these rudimentary efforts may be embarrassing to the artist, they can provide raw material and inspiration for new pieces.

In the electronic environment, you can easily borrow from old drawings. Images created previously can be copied and pasted into new backgrounds to create new graphic effects.

Save all your drawings; an idea turned down today may be picked up tomorrow.

This drawing was created a few years ago. We hung on to it, because you never know when a graphic may prove useful in a new context, as demonstrated on the following page.

Copying an image from an existing piece of electronic artwork saves time and effort.

A recent situation called for an illustration of a ship in a bottle. By copying the image of the ship from our existing artwork, we have conserved time and effort.

You should also think in terms of your old artwork when creating new graphics. Do you have anything on disk that can be reworked? Cataloging your old artwork can be very useful in this respect. When you've finished a graphic, print an extra copy, label it with its file name, and toss it in a notebook or folder designated for sketches. Browsing through a folder of artwork is much easier and more accurate than trying to remember what sketches and final drafts you have on disk.

The process of creating a computer graphic consists of four steps: First, determine your purpose for creating the graphic and develop a concept. Then, generate hard copies of your ideas by sketching them either with a pencil on paper or by using a painting application. The latter method is preferable, since it provides you with an opportunity to practice creating computer art in a casual setting, without having to concentrate on a polished finished product. Next, select a favorite sketch and develop it into a final illustration in your drawing program. Finally, save your graphic to disk, and catalog it for possible future consideration.

The final step in the graphic process, saving a file to disk, is straightforward. In most drawing programs, you save an image by choosing a menu command, a practice familiar even to those with limited computer experience. The first step, developing a concept, is probably not foreign or intimidating either. If you've worked in advertising, visual media, printing, or any related field, you may have been involved in formulating graphic ideas that were later transformed into illustrations by a staff artist. Even if you have never worked with an artist or marketing committee, you have probably imagined visual ideas that could be worked into drawings. Something as elemental as a dream, for example, is fundamentally a visualization of a concept, an idea entirely your own.

For most non-artists, steps two and three are the most difficult, since they involve actual drawing. If we were to end our discussion here, you would understand how to create a graphic without knowing how to draw, severely limiting your potential success. For this reason, most of this book is devoted to analyzing the process of drawing and then applying our knowledge to common categories of graphics using a typical drawing application.

Sketching initial ideas and creating a final draft are steps in the graphic process that require drawing technique.

Examining drawing technique

Whether you are using pencil and paper or mouse and keyboard, the effectiveness of your graphic depends on your drawing technique. *Technique* refers to the knowledge and tools that an artist uses to create an illustration.

Most artists are educated in form, scale, proportion, depth, and related subjects. This knowledge of drawing theory guides an artist through the creation of an illustration, providing a basis on which to make decisions about what goes where and how things should look.

An artist's tools include pencils, paint, brushes, paper, and canvas. In a drawing program, similar tools are accessed by clicking icons in an electronic toolbox. An understanding of the purposes as well as the possible uses of tools will enhance your technique.

You can learn to draw by developing a successful technique, regardless of any precon- ceptions of natural ability.

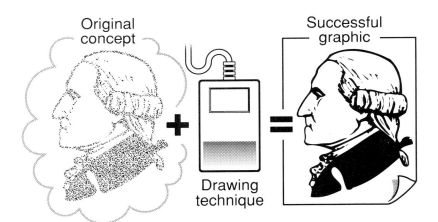

An understanding of theory and tools forms the foundation of a successful drawing technique, which provides the knowledge required to move your mouse in the directions and distances necessary to convert a mental image into a visual form.

By gaining an understanding of both drawing theory and software tools, a computer artist assembles an electronic drawing technique—the essential link between formulating a graphic concept and expressing it identifiably on paper.

Technique differentiates those who can draw from those who cannot. By developing a successful technique, a person can learn to draw, regardless of any preconceptions of natural ability.

The qualifier in this discussion is the artist's style. Any two contemporary artists may have the same educational background and access to identical tools. However, one artist's technique may be less successful than the other's simply because of a difference in artistic style. In this sense, style dictates not only the appearance of an artist's work, but the manner in which it was created as well.

Sketching initial ideas and creating a final draft require a successful drawing technique. As we have indicated in the figure, a knowledge of drawing theory plus an understanding of software tools, modified by your personal artistic style, is the formula for technique.

Drawing ability is the combined result of knowing how to draw and knowing what to draw with.

Being able to draw is therefore the integration of knowing how to draw and knowing what to draw with. As you might suspect, these topics are so large that our first four chapters are devoted to aspects of drawing technique. Chapter 2 is an in-depth examination of drawing theory, including form, scale, proportion, and depth. In Chapter 3, we examine the tools and menu commands available in most drawing applications. In Chapter 4, we point out some possible uses of these software tools.

That leaves only artistic style, the modifier of drawing technique. Style is a considerably smaller, less tangible subject. We will discuss style for the remainder of this chapter.

Personal artistic style

Every professional artist has a distinctive style. Each drawing created by an artist is immediately recognizable as typical of that artist's work. You are probably familiar with many artists' styles even without knowing their names. Such familiarity provides a link between artist and viewer that helps win the viewer over to your product or idea.

A distinctive style serves a product or company more effectively than a generic style, regardless of the technical quality of the artwork. Since a viewer's affinity for a particular style may blind him or her to a flawed drawing technique, every artist should strive to develop a distinctive and consistent personal artistic style.

A distinctive artistic style serves a product or company more effectively than a generic style, even when the technique is flawless.

Each of these four drawings depicts George Washington, yet each differs from the others in one or more stylistic respects. The first George is robust and confident; the second is stiff and impersonal; the third appears carved in stone; and the fourth is rendered as a silhouette. All are drawings of the same man, and three are drawn from similar angles. Nonetheless, each is clearly distinguishable from the others. Each is obviously drawn by a dfferent artist and possesses a unique quality and character.

If you are just beginning to learn to draw, you probably have yet to develop an artistic style. The easiest solution is to copy drawing styles of established artists. Avoid the mistake of trying to emulate the style of a *single* favorite artist. You may be far too successful! If your style is identical to that of another artist, you limit your creative development. A better idea is to borrow from many artists, carefully scrutinizing their work and borrowing only the few techniques from each that you find valuable.

For business reasons, you may wish to counterfeit the style of another artist. Rather than forsaking your personal style altogether, try to reach a compromise. To please your business interests, you may work elements of another artist's style into your drawing, while at the same time displaying enough of your own style to further your personal goals and artistic development.

You can produce interesting effects by copying the content of one graphic and the style of another.

Besides helping an audience to identify your work, your style will play a decisive role in improving the quality of your work. We mentioned earlier that personal style modifies the way in which an artist applies knowledge of drawing theory and software tools. By working yourself into your artwork, you also work yourself into your technique. If you take the time to develop a personal artistic style, you will increase your artistic knowledge as well.

———————

Drawing technique is a qualifying determinant in the graphic process—if you can't draw, you can't sketch and you can't create a final illustration. As we have discussed, a knowledge of drawing theory and an understanding of software tools are two key elements in developing a successful drawing technique. Thorough examinations of these topics are contained in the next three chapters. The third key element, your personal artistic style, enables you to adeptly display your command of technique. The time you spend developing a style will enhance your experience, increase your knowledge of drawing theory and software tools, and solidify your understanding of the graphic process in general.

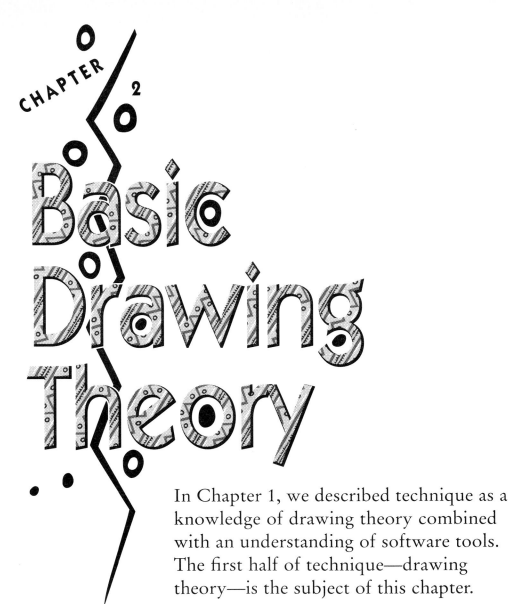

CHAPTER 2

Basic Drawing Theory

In Chapter 1, we described technique as a knowledge of drawing theory combined with an understanding of software tools. The first half of technique—drawing theory—is the subject of this chapter.

In the same way that an understanding of tools can be considered an artist's practical knowledge, drawing theory is the sum of an artist's academic knowledge. For example, because of his or her understanding of tools, an artist knows that a pencil creates graphite lines when rubbed against paper. But if the artist wants to draw a graphite line that represents a duck or a tree or a house, he or she must rely on drawing theory. An artist uses theory to determine how lines should be drawn, how shapes should be formed, and how colors should be applied.

Drawing theory may be analyzed as many separate elements, which we will call building blocks. Each building block may or may not be used to create a particular graphic. This chapter focuses on each building block both individually and in relation to others.

The building blocks that make a successful technique are:

Drawing theory determines how tools can be used to represent images.

1. *Presentation...*
How to draw graphics professionally.

2. *Form...*
How to accurately record the shape of an image.

3. *Scale...*
How large or small to create objects with respect to each other.

4. *Proportion...*
How large or small to create each portion of a single object in relation to other portions.

5. *Depth...*
How to create the illusion of three dimensions on a flat piece of paper by using perspective, detail, and shades of gray.

6. *Volume...*
How to determine a source of light to create highlights, shadows, and reflections on an object.

7. *Color . . .*
How colors blend and interact and how to apply them when using a color monitor or printing in color.

Presenting your ideas

Drawing realistic forms

Scaling multiple objects

Determining proportions

Demonstrating depth

Representing volume

Adding color

The most
advanced
drawing
technique will
include
a knowledge of
all seven
building blocks.

The seven building blocks are displayed in order and size of importance. Throughout this chapter, we will use these icons to highlight discussions of corresponding topics.

The earliest building blocks are the most essential. For example, you might create a simple drawing using only your knowledge of the first building block—presentation. A more advanced graphic would also incorporate form. However, a drawing cannot successfully demonstrate depth without also successfully demonstrating proportion, scale, form, and presentation. The most advanced graphic will incorporate all seven building blocks.

Presenting your ideas

A viewer or audience may love or hate your work regardless of its technical merit. In fact, a theoretically atrocious drawing can be very popular if the "feeling" is right. We call this intangible quality of a graphic its *presentation*.

The purpose of a professional presentation is to hide a drawing's flaws and enhance its strengths. In this sense, we can best define presentation by separating it into two elements:

1. *Appropriateness*—does your drawing attract or repel viewers?

2. *Appeal*—is your drawing likable?

Presentation deals exclusively with how your graphic affects its audience.

Neither of these elements serves to judge if your drawing is successful. Presentation deals exclusively with how your graphic affects its viewer, regardless of the graphic's technical qualities. In other words, presentation determines first impressions. Either a viewer likes your drawing immediately or the drawing fails to fulfill its purpose. In the world of commercial art, there is no middle ground. After all, you can't dismiss a viewer's lack of enthusiasm by attributing it to your own artistic genius.

A drawing that is both appropriate and appealing elicits a good first impression, even if it looks like it was drawn by a four-year-old. For example, a typical four-year-old draws with big fat crayons on newsprint. Because the child has no knowledge of drawing theory and a limited understanding of his or her tools, the finished product is usually technically worthless. Nonetheless, if you saw this child's drawing on a holiday greeting card, you might think it very endearing. The presentation is appropriate because a greeting card is a light-hearted, informal message. The presentation is appealing because holidays are typically nostalgic times when people enjoy being re-minded of their childhoods.

By contrast, a drawing that is neither appropriate nor appealing elicits a poor first impression. If you went on vacation to a foreign country and discovered that the currency had a child's drawings printed on it, you might board the next flight home. There is nothing childlike about economic security, and such play money might appeal only to counterfeiters.

For the next few pages, we will concentrate on appropriateness and appeal individually.

Appropriateness:
Drawing for your audience

Even the most expertly crafted drawing can fail to consider its audi-ence. By considering the suitability of your graphic concept in terms of how it will affect a viewer, you address the most important element in creating a successful drawing—appropriateness.

Suppose that when creating our dog food advertisement in Chapter 1, we had decided to present a cat eating the dog food. No matter how well we had drawn the cat, it would not have impressed dog owners, for the simple reason that they buy dog food for their dogs to eat, not for cats. Our audience would have ignored the draw-ing from the outset.

Appropriateness is the fundamental manner in which a concept is conveyed.

Appropriateness is therefore the fundamental manner in which a concept is conveyed. It determines whether a graphic is noticed or neglected. If a graphic is uninteresting or offensive to your intended viewer, then its presentation is inappropriate.

Suppose we want to draw a simple wooden doll for a general audience. Above are three examples of possible final drafts. Each drawing is similar in style, but presented differently. The first doll is presented as a shapely barmaid, the second is presented undergoing electroshock therapy, and the third is presented as a little girl with a bow in her hair. For very specific audiences and environments, the first two dolls might be appropriate. But only the last doll can be considered appropriate for a general audience.

An appropriate drawing gets noticed; an inappropriate drawing may be ignored. Hence, appropriateness is the primary determinant of first impressions. If you don't draw for your audience, they aren't going to pay attention to your work. When sketching your first ideas, concentrate on a presentation that will immediately grab the attention of your viewers. If your audience likes dogs, represent your idea appropriately by including a dog.

Appropriateness determines whether a graphic is noticed or neglected.

An appropriate drawing hooks its viewer. That's half of what presentation is about. But you have to do more than make an audience look at your drawing; you also have to inspire them to *like* it. To be effective, a graphic must be appealing as well as appropriate. The following text explains why.

The importance of appeal

Appeal is instrumental to the success of a graphic due to the basic relationship between your graphic and any surrounding text. By its nature, a graphic is visually more entertaining than a typical block of text. The visual appeal of graphics account for their abundance throughout printed advertisements and commercial text.

You must inspire your audience to look at a drawing and to like it.

A graphic is exciting because:

1. It represents an idea intuitively. A viewer immediately absorbs the general idea of a graphic subliminally and notices more subtle details after only a brief gaze.

2. It visually resembles something encountered in daily life.

3. It stands out from a sea of gray blocks of text and demands viewer attention.

Text is dull because:

1. It defines an idea through a series of abstract marks and symbols. Few readers absorb ideas from the written word faster than from an effectual graphic.

2. It visually resembles nothing, except countless other gray blocks of text.

3. It blends in with the rest of a printed page. A typical block of text does not jump out at the reader.

If viewers
like your
graphic, they
will be
more receptive
to its message.

*She smiled
secretly.*

This example demonstrates how much more exciting a graphic can be than a block of text, even when they represent the same idea.

The fact that a graphic stands out more than text can be as much a disadvantage as a strength. An audience will identify an unappealing graphic more quickly and with more certainty than unappealing text. After all, you must *read* a body of text to determine its presentation. Bad graphic presentation is readily apparent, even blatant.

The appeal of a graphic is therefore important because a graphic is the most prominent element on a printed page. If an audience likes your graphic, then they will be more receptive to its message as well as to that of the text accompanying the graphic.

Next, we lay some guidelines for creating an appealing graphic and ensuring that your idea receives a popular review.

Creating appealing artwork

If you were to position two appealing graphics side by side and scrutinize them, you would probably discover that they had both similar and dissimilar strengths and weaknesses. There are no proven rights or wrongs for any one artistic style. Ultimately, you'll have to experiment to discover those strengths that are most easily integrated into your personal style. We can, however, offer some guidelines that should help improve the general appeal of the work you create using a standard drawing application.

To achieve an appealing graphic, we recommend these guidelines:

1. *Draw large.* Fill your allotted space generously. A scrawny drawing surrounded awkwardly by too much white space and filled with squashed, unidentifiable details is usually not visually appealing. If a drawing turns out to be too big for its space, you can always reduce it after completion. (Enlarging a too-small graphic is not necessarily the solution, since this may enhance awkward details.)

2. *Draw elegantly.* Represent an image powerfully, or delicately, or athletically, or in some other positive posture that fits the circumstance. Exaggerate aspects of your image that you think will impress your viewers; de-emphasize those that might be disagreeable or even offensive. Represent an image the way you think your viewer will most like to see it.

3. *Maintain a consistent style.* For example, don't stylize one portion of an image and then make another portion very realistic. By drawing inconsistently, you draw unwanted attention to your style and diminish the effect of your illustration as a whole.

The three guidelines to creating an appealing graphic are to draw large, elegantly, and consistently.

This drawing lacks appeal because it violates all three guidelines for an appealing presentation. First, it's scrawny. It fills so little space that the surrounding text overwhelms it. Second, it is not represented in a positive posture. An overstuffed bird wavering on spongy legs, thrusting its bill into a spotted mess of seed, is unlikely to elicit a positive reaction from an audience. Third, the style of execution is inconsistent. Lines become thicker and thinner arbitrarily. The body of the bird is round and polished, while the wings, bill, and legs hang uselessly like flimsy bits of tissue.

This drawing depicts the same bird shown in our previous figure. It is not drawn any better than the first drawing, yet it is more appealing because the presentation is better. First of all, it's larger: it fills the page better and therefore appears stronger, more impressive. Second, the bird is standing upright. This change in posture makes a more dynamic illustration, suggesting a bird ready to leap into flight. Third,

Developing a Successful Drawing Technique

the style of the graphic is consistent. The legs are represented as simple straight lines, more in keeping with the simplified body of the bird. The ground is squared off and the seeds are rendered more uniformly. The result is a very appealing graphic.

A graphic dominates text on the printed page. Any element that draws so much attention had better be good. Your audience is likely to forgive a graphic's boldness, or even admire it, if the graphic appeals to them. By following the three rules for creating an appealing presentation—draw large, draw elegantly, and draw consistently—you increase the likelihood that your audience will like your drawing. And if they like your drawing, your viewers will be more receptive to your message and more likely to read any surrounding text.

Any element that draws as much attention as a graphic must appeal to its audience.

A first impression is often the only impression an audience will form about your work. The manner in which you present a graphic invariably determines that first impression.

For example, suppose you want to give a gift to a friend. By wrapping the gift, you are presenting it in a format that you know, from experience, will impress your friend. The same is true for an illustration. When you consider your audience by drawing appropriately and appeal to the audience by using our three guidelines—drawing large, elegantly, and consistently—you are wrapping your graphic in a professional presentation, one which will impress your viewer. Even if you can't draw, you can achieve an appropriate and appealing presentation. And if you can draw, your drawing will fail to convey your message without a proper presentation.

Presentation is our first building block for developing a successful drawing technique because it is the most essential. However, presentation alone is like wrapping a stick of chewing gum in a refrigerator box; packaging requires content. This leads to our next building block, form. A realistic form ensures that an audience won't be disappointed once they get beyond the presentation.

Drawing realistic forms

As we mentioned in Chapter 1, our primary goal in drawing is to present an image that clearly conveys specific visual information to the viewer. Often we can accomplish this by creating an outline that follows the basic *form* of an object rather than portraying the object in full detail with shading. This approach saves time and hones your drawing skills.

To present the form of any object, we may rely on simple straight and curved lines that are easily created and modified. Although outlines do not appear around forms in real life, we often use lines as a graphic tool to define the edges of objects. For example, with the possible exception of wrinkles, no lines clearly trace the features of your face. However, if you were creating a self-portrait, you might create one line to express the shape of your nose, another to represent an eyebrow, another for your mouth, and so on, with all lines enclosed in a larger outline representing the form of your face.

Whether you are trying to record a simple or complex image, start by outlining its basic form.

Here we have two versions of an egg sitting in a grassy lawn. In the first image, the form of the egg is expressed realistically using shading and gray values, as it would be in a photograph or a painting. In the second image, we express the form of the egg as an oval outline. In spite of their differences, both drawings accurately demonstrate the form of an egg. But obviously, the outlined image was much easier to create and required less skill and effort than the shaded image.

Notice the grass in our two representations of an egg. When drawing the grass for our outline drawing, we could have created a bunch of small lines or even tried to trace the form of each individual blade. Instead, we saved both time and effort by demonstrating only the form of the grass. Although we have simplified it to its bare essentials, the grass remains identifiable.

Whether you are trying to record a simple or complex image, start by outlining its basic form. Outlines not only allow you to represent the image quickly, but they may also serve as a starting point should you decide to add more detail.

The following discussion is designed to help you to learn how to quickly read the basic form of an object and draw it on screen.

New artists often run into problems when they draw the way they presume an object to look, ignoring its real form.

Recording forms accurately

The best way to learn to represent form accurately is to draw from real life or from photographs. This way, you don't have to remember or imagine how something looks. The biggest problem of most new artists is that they draw the way they presume objects to look, ignoring the real forms. If you frequently consult your model while drawing—concentrating on drawing an object as it is, not as you think it is—you will have more success.

Here are three experiments you can try while sketching in a painting program to improve both your drawing skill and your knowledge of form. All are intended as experiments only; they should not be adopted as permanent drawing habits.

1. While sketching, keep your eyes on your real-life or photographic model. Never look at your computer screen.

   This is similar to typing without looking at the keyboard. You are forced to rely exclusively on your model for form information rather than making up forms based on the evolving structure of your drawing. Since it is often difficult to remember what you have drawn and it is impossible to know where you should begin and end lines, your completed sketch will probably be a mess. Only after you have finished your sketch should you look at your computer screen, adding details and making corrections based on what you have drawn. Your increased knowledge of the real form of your model will also help in this correction phase.

2. If you are sketching from a photo, turn it upside down, and try drawing it that way.

   An object is much less familiar when viewed upside down. You will be less tempted to make up a form as you draw if you have no preconception of what the form should look like. Once your sketch is completed, rotate the entire image right side up. You'll be surprised by how good it looks!

It is easiest to record the actual forms of an image if you draw from a model and refer to it often.

3. Fill your entire screen with black using your paint program's fill tool. Then work backward, drawing with your pencil tool to subtract lines that should not be there.

   This is similar to whittling wood. You essentially carve away parts of your drawing that shouldn't be there, rather than adding lines and shapes. Like the previous experiment, this unfamiliar drawing method forces you to further examine the form of the object.

As we mentioned earlier, these are only experiments; they are not intended to be substituted for your normal drawing procedure. However, after practicing these experiments, you will find that it is easier to record the actual forms of images if you sketch from a model and refer to it as often as possible.

By learning to record realistic forms, you can effectively communicate your idea to a viewer without wasting a lot of drawing time. Simple, accurate forms are easily recognizable by most viewers; inaccurate forms, no matter how detailed or elegantly shaded, are frequently confusing.

Simple, accurate forms are easily recognizable to most viewers.

These are two representations of a fish. It may be difficult to recognize the first image, even though it is very detailed, because its form is highliy inaccurate. Obviously, the artist did not consult a model. The second image required less time to draw but more accurately reflects the outline of a fish. The simple outlines of the image give it a clean, crisp appearance.

An audience recognizes accurate forms and is confused by inaccurate forms. Accurate forms don't have to be complex; in fact, they may created using only one or two lines. To ensure that your outlines are accurate, always draw from a model, whether real-life or photographed.

An image is most recognizable when you represent the form of the object accurately. But unfortunately, the real world can sometimes be a little dull. For example, the fish on the right of our previous figure may be easily recognizable, but it isn't as exciting as the image on the left. Does realism have to be boring? What is the purpose of drawing if the best you can do is no better than real life?

With art, you can often represent an image more interestingly than it occurs in real life. In fact, one of the primary functions of art is to enhance nature. In the next few pages, we discuss methods for enhancing reality that involve the manipulation of form.

Stylizing form

Only after you understand how to create realistic outlines can you manipulate form to enliven an illustration. We offer two methods that may be used by intermediate artists to enhance form. The first of these is *stylization*.

To stylize an image is to represent it as a series of geometric shapes, often simplifying the image in the process. As long as these shapes are based on realistic forms, you can achieve fantastic drawings that remain recognizable.

With experience, you can stylize the outlines of an object to enhance an illustration.

Stylization is a perfect extension of your drawing program's capabilities.

In each graphic above, we have used lines and shapes to express selected details of a lion and its environment. Each drawing stylizes the form without obscuring it. For example, while much of the first lion is drawn naturalistically, the mane and background employ stylized linear and floral patterns. We eliminated much of the detail in the second lion,

relying exclusively on black and white shapes to represent the image. And in the third graphic, we have represented the image entirely as geometric shapes filled with a pattern of perpendicular lines. The forms of all three lions, however, are equally accurate, despite their different stylizations.

Stylizing details in the outline of an object produces an exciting image that enhances realism without departing from it entirely. In addition, geometric images are a perfect extention of your computer's capabilities. Straight lines, squares, rectangles, and other polygons are among the easiest objects to create in a drawing program. Stylization is one way of expanding your working knowledge of form that is particularly applicable in an electronic environment. Using methods that are suited to your computer allows you to have fun with a drawing and translate that enthusiasm to your viewer.

The second method for enhancing reality does not involve altering form, but rather involves organizing it. We call this method composition.

Because we rarely see a fluid composition in real life, it is an effective means of enhancing reality in artwork.

Composition: The consistent flow of form

As we mentioned, reality can be dull. In the case of our lion, we altered reality by stylizing the many small forms that make up the animal and its environment. We simplified the image to its most essential details, we made the image more geometric, and we enhanced the image by adding an unusual pattern. But sometimes, the effectiveness of a drawing is less dependent on the numerous small forms of an object than on its overall form. How do the various details of your model relate to each other? If you are drawing a face, how does one eye relate to the other? If you are drawing a person, how do the arms relate to the torso and the legs? This overall sense of form is *composition*.

Developing a Successful Drawing Technique

Think of your drawing as a river. A river that flows in a straight line or a consistent arc allows water to pass through it more quickly than a river that winds back and forth, crimping about small nooks and pools. Likewise, your drawing will be more effective if it follows a straight line or consistent arc. Since fluid composition is rarely seen in real life, it is an effective means of enhancing reality in your artwork. Like water in a river, a concept flows most quickly from artist to audience through a linear drawing.

Both of these cartoon athletes are reasonably accurate in form. Yet the punter on the left appears awkward, scrunched up, as if he is neither powerful nor skilled. Although a person might actually kick a ball while assuming this position, there is little reason to represent an athlete in this way. You might prefer to show him in the stance on the right. This guy seems to be knocking the football out of the stands! His form moves in a consistent direction, thus the composition is linear.

The concept of a graphic flows most quickly through a linear composition.

Often, linear composition requires that you alter the form of an image slightly from its real-life or photographic model. In such a case, you might find it helpful to first draw the object accurately. Then re-arrange the details of the object using the various drawing program commands that we'll discuss in the next chapter. In this way, you may alter composition without disturbing the form of an object.

Composition is based on form. Forms are the outlines of various parts of an object; composition is the outline of the object as a whole. Composition is an element of drawing theory useful to the intermediate artist, because only after understanding form can you master composition.

———————◆—▪◉▪—◆———————

Accurately outlining the basic forms of an object conveys your idea quickly and clearly, without requiring numerous details or complicated effects. Representing an image in a linear composition increases the effectiveness of your graphic by enhancing reality. Together, a knowledge of form and composition can be used to turn scrawls into elegant line drawings.

Form is a theoretical tool. A knowledge of form allows an artist to communicate an idea to a viewer. Our next building block—scale—is also theoretical tool. A knowledge of scale provides additional visual possibilities for an artist.

Scaling multiple objects

In the first section of this chapter, we mentioned that enlarging the overall size of a graphic increases its appeal. But within a single graphic, you may also increase or reduce the size of one object in relation to other objects. For example, suppose that you want to create an illustration depicting a giant and a dwarf. Naturally, you would draw the giant much larger than the dwarf to communicate their considerable difference in height. Relative sizing of various objects within a single graphic is called *scaling*.

It is often useful for an artist to scale individual objects in a graphic to different sizes. In fact, contrast in scale can be extremely useful to indicate one or more of the following visual themes:

1. *Actual size differences.* Some objects are larger than others. For example, a giant is bigger than a dwarf.

2. *Distance.* An object in the foreground appears larger than a similarly sized or even larger object in the background. If a dwarf was very close to us and a giant was very far away, the dwarf would look bigger than the giant.

3. *Importance.* Scale can be used to highlight important visual concepts or accompanying text. If you wanted to show that dwarves constitute a larger percentage of world population than giants, you could exaggerate the relative sizes of the dwarf and the giant.

4. *Drama.* Very large objects and very small objects can be coupled to produce dramatic results. By increasing the scale of our giant tenfold, we elevate our drawing from dwarf with giant to Jack and the Beanstalk!

Each of the four effects of scaling is explained and examined in the following pages.

Scale objects to different sizes to communicate various physical and abstract relationships.

Indicating actual size differences

The easiest way to begin learning scale is to draw objects according to their actual size relationships. For example, if you were drawing an illustration featuring a gray whale and a guppy fish, the whale should be bigger. In fact, you should probably represent the whale hundreds or even thousands of times larger than the guppy, since such a scale accurately demonstrates the physical size difference between the two animals. Conversely, drawing a monster guppy fish towering over a minuscule whale will probably confuse your audience unless the idea is compatible with a visual theme or story line.

 The easiest way to begin learning scale is to draw objects according to their actual size relationships.

This size relationship between an eagle and a killer whale is unrealistic. Unless the killer whale is supposed to be a very small baby, it should be scaled up to an accurate size representation and removed from the eagle's tallons.

When creating multiple objects in the same graphic, pay careful attention to their relative sizes. Objects that are represented accurately with respect to each other are more easily recognizable; realistic scaling will ensure that your graphic is understood by a general audience.

Do you always have to draw objects to the same scale? After all, when you look out the window of a plane, a car on the ground looks smaller than your finger. You know your finger to be considerably smaller than a car, however, so there must be some instances when scale can be altered.

Distance: Scaling between foreground and background

In real life, you see objects scaled in proportion to their distance from you. As an example, hold your finger an arm's length from your face. As you slowly move your finger closer, it consumes a larger portion of your field of vision, thus appearing larger. In this way, your finger can be made to seem as large as a distant car or building. If you move it away, it takes up less of your field of vision and appears to shrink. The size that you perceive an object to be depends on your distance from that object.

Objects are enlarged or reduced to indicate their proximity to the viewer.

Here we have drawn a bowler and her ball at the same scale, sized in normal relationship to each other. Both the ball and bowler appear to be in the foreground of our graphic.

Since scale is not constant in real life, you should alter the scale of objects in your drawings as well. Objects should be exaggerated or downplayed in scale to indicate their proximity to the viewer. An easy first experiment is to consider your drawing as consisting of only a foreground and a background. Draw all foreground objects at one large scale; draw all background objects at a smaller scale. (If more than one object exists in either the foreground or background, those objects should be scaled according to their actual size relationships.)

Relatively small objects appear to be at the back of a graphic, large objects seem to be close up.

Because the bowling ball is drawn at an exaggerated size, it seems to be rushing at us. Although the ball is huge compared to the bowler, the graphic remains identifiable because we perceive the ball as being closer to us. In addition, having both a foreground (the bowling ball) and a background (the bowler) enhances the reality of the graphic by giving it the appearance of depth (a topic discussed more fully later in this chapter).

Developing a Successful Drawing Technique

If you want to show that one portion of a graphic is in front of another portion, increase its scale. Likewise, if you want an object to appear behind others, decrease its scale. Relatively small objects appear to be at the back of a graphic, large objects look close up.

When you scale objects according to their actual size relationships or according to their distances from the viewer, you are using scale realistically. But as we mentioned in our discussion of form, it is possible to use scale to enhance reality and increase viewer interest. Like stylization and composition, using scale to indicate importance is a method for enhancing reality without diminishing viewer recognition.

Scaling to indicate importance

Rather than representing objects realistically, we can use scale to represent things idealistically. In this way, scale highlights the relative importance of images. Large objects tend to look formidable and impressive; smaller objects look less important, more incidental.

Scaling for importance imparts a message without confusing the viewer.

As an example, consider a graphic accompanying a story in a business journal. The story is about how foreign small-car manufacturers are taking a bite out of the luxury car industry. A huge compact is shown running over a tiny Cadillac. Although a compact is a much smaller car than a Cadillac, the graphic is recognizable as a deliberate distortion of reality. Scaling for importance allows you to impart a message without confusing your viewer.

In this sense, unusual contrasts in scale can be applied to indicate differences in popularity, skill, intelligence, strength, competitiveness, productivity, quality, durability, value, potential, notoriety, intensity, and growth. Even negative or questionable attributes or behaviors, such as risk, opportunism, takeovers, terrorism, deficit spending, and substance abuse, can be illustrated by distortions in scaling.

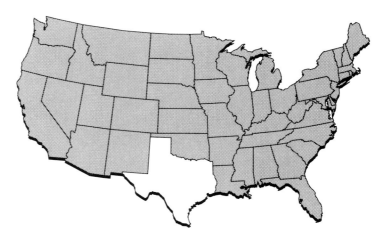

Here, all 48 continental United States are shown at the same scale, each state sized accurately in relation to the others. We have subtly emphasized the state of Texas by shading it white and shading all other states gray.

When drawing an object, consider its importance in relation to other objects in your graphic.

By increasing the scale of Texas, as well as deforming and deleting neighboring states, we attach special importance to the Lone Star State. Viewers familiar with the U.S. will understand that this is not how Texas really looks, but that the graphic emphasizes some aspect in which Texas excels.

Developing a Successful Drawing Technique

Use scale to guide your viewer. Incidental graphic elements should be small. In the previous figure, most states except Texas are drawn to a consistent scale, since their only purpose is to serve as a contrast to the enormity of the Lone Star State. If every state was large, Texas would not stand out and would therefore seem much less important.

When drawing an object, consider its importance in relation to other objects in your graphic. If you want one object to attract more attention than another, increase its scale. If you want to downplay an element's importance, decrease its scale. And if you want all objects to share the same importance, keep their sizes realistic.

The final effect of scaling also departs from reality, but not as obviously as the ones we have already mentioned. Rather, differences in scale are exaggerated to produce dramatic results that increase viewer attention without imparting a specific message.

Scaling for drama

Huge size differences between objects can provide very impressive and dramatic results. For example, one reason the redwoods of northern California are so popular is because of their immense size relative to other trees. In the same way, vast contrast in scale increases a graphic's effectiveness. This is especially true if a very large object is positioned close to a very small object, whose size is readily identifiable. A viewer should be able to immediately recognize the small object as something that is not commonly associated with smallness, such as a animal, car, house, and so on. The small object thus demonstrates the immensity of the larger element.

A small object may be used for contrast, demonstrating the immensity of a large object.

A dramatic
illustration
contrasts a
human being
against the
grandness of the
natural world.

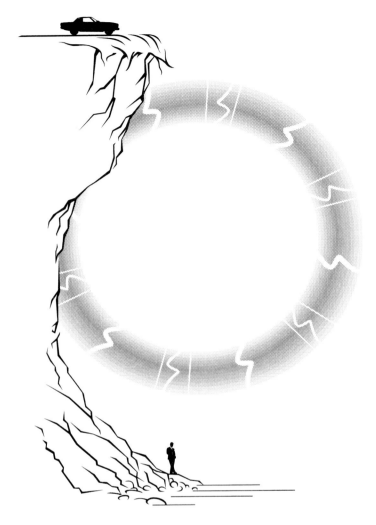

Natural monuments make for dramatic illustrations, but their size cannot be gauged by an audience without adding a small object for scale reference. In this graphic, we have added the images of a man and a car in order to demonstrate the size of a rocky cliff. In general, while few viewers have preconceptions regarding the height of a particular cliff, they can readily understand the size of a human or an automobile. These familiar, consistently sized elements provide a tangible reference from which the viewer can infer the size of the cliff.

Developing a Successful Drawing Technique

Whenever you represent grandiose landmarks or dramatic natural monuments, scale can play an important role. Position a small, familiar object alongside or atop the landmark to demonstrate its largeness and drama. By introducing a small object, your large object seems larger, and your drawing seems more expertly crafted and interesting.

———————◆◆◆———————

Scaling is a useful method for enhancing your graphics. But keep in mind that it is useful only when a graphic contains more than one element. Although the effectiveness of a single-object graphic can be improved by increasing the size of the image, it is more a function of presentation, which we discussed earlier.

Any time your graphic contains more than one object, consider whether some objects should be scaled to indicate the relative size, to demonstrate distance, to highlight importance, or to increase dramatic impact.

The fourth building block of drawing theory is proportion. Like scale, proportion can be used to indicate several visual themes. But proportion is a more advanced theoretical tool than scale, and its impact on a graphic is more subtle than that of scale.

When a graphic contains more than one object, consider how each should be scaled.

Determining proportions

We have discussed how the scaling of various objects can enhance a graphic. Another form of scaling can be used to affect the appearance of a single object. Details and features of an object can be scaled independently of each other within the single element. This technique is known as altering the *proportions* of an object.

For example, a man named Cyrano is unhappy about his looks. He fears the object of his affections (call her Roxanne) finds him unattractive because his nose is too long. He hires a plastic surgeon to reduce the size of his nose by an operation. In effect, he has altered the proportions of his face to enhance his appearance. As an artist, you can likewise alter the proportions of objects in your drawing to enhance its appearance.

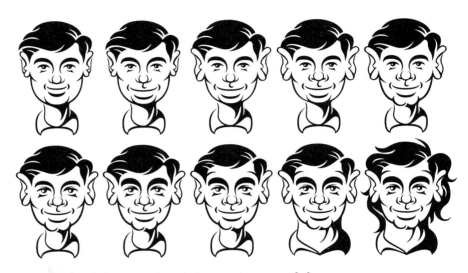

A single image may be made to look very different by altering its proportions.

Each of these ten heads is a caricature of the same person. The only difference is in the proportion of the features. Starting with the top left face and working across the rows, we enlarge one feature at a time. First we enlarge the mouth, then the ears, the nose, the chin, the eyes, the eyebrows, the forehead (giving our man a receding hairline), the neck, and finally we lengthen the hair. The result is that the last face looks very different from the first. Notice, however, that we never alter the size of the head itself; the same basic framework is retained in all views.

It is often useful to consider proportions of various features within an element. Proportional differences and oddities may serve several purposes:

1. To accurately represent the proportional differences that exist within an object. Some objects are short and fat, others are tall and thin, others have big ears, and so on.

2. To make an object more interesting. Sometimes reality isn't as entertaining as fiction. By enhancing reality, you can produce more visually interesting results.

3. To force visual relationships between objects. If two or more objects in a drawing share an unusually large or small feature, they have an obvious relationship that lends harmony to your work.

Each of these three results of altering proportions is discussed in the following pages.

The proportions of an image have a profound effect on how it is interpreted by a viewer.

Accurately representing proportional differences

As we demonstrated for scale, the easiest way to begin learning about proportions is to draw various features of an object according to the actual size relationships between them. For example, a snake has a long, thin, slick body. If you create a short, fat snake with long fur, you will probably confuse your audience, since these proportions are inconsistent with the snakes your viewers are used to seeing.

When drawing the elephant on the left, we paid specific attention to the proportions of the animal's face, representing the size relationships of various features as realistically as possible. The trunk is long, the ears are large, the eyes are small, and so on. When drawing the creature on the right, we ignored the proportions of an elephant's face. The trunk is short, the ear are small, and the eyes bulge. We even added a long neck and a tall forehead. The result is an unfamiliar animal that bears little resemblance to an elephant.

Always pay careful attention to the relative size of details of an object. When its features are represented accurately with respect to each other, an object can be recognized more easily, thus ensuring that your graphic is widely understood by a general audience.

Once again, however, reality is not always what your viewers want to see. Once you understand the real proportions of an object, you may enhance an illustration without confusing your audience by exaggerating proportions in the same way as we described for form and scaling.

Making an object more interesting

By altering the proportions of an object, you can improve on reality, especially when a real-life or photographic model is flat or uninteresting. You may even find that exaggerating a proportion or two adds power or grace to a graphic.

Suppose that you are creating an illustration for an article in the company newsletter featuring a dynamic duo of the month. These two employees saved the company from crisis, and you want to create a portrait that will inspire the admiration of their colleagues. Unfortunately, neither of our heroes are particularly attractive. If you draw them as they really appear, fellow workers may be more bewildered by their abilities than impressed. By exaggerating those features that are heroic and downplaying those that are less heroic, you alter their proportions in a way that benefits the article.

But how do you know what proportions you can exaggerate without confusing your audience? The rule of thumb here is to avoid altering those proportions that help a viewer to identify an image. Since people recognize an elephant by its long trunk, you should exaggerate the trunk by lengthening it, but not by shortening it. If you want to exaggerate portions of a fish, make its fins bigger or smaller, but you shouldn't remove the fins entirely or substitute legs.

Exaggerating elegant features and down-playing homely details can enhance your graphic's message.

You may augment reality by altering a proportion or two. The fish on the left is accurately drawn, but lacks flair. By subtly enlarging its fins, gills, and scales, as well as enhancing its mouth and eyes, we produce the more visually enter-taining fish on the right. With very little effort, we have developed our fish almost to cartoon proportions, without overwhelming the simplicity that marked our original fish or detracting from viewer recognition of its "fishy" appearance.

To make an object more interesting, you may exaggerate appropriate proportions. Just be careful that your exaggerations don't obscure the object's identity so much that viewers no longer recognize it.

Our next method uses similar proportions in separate objects to link the objects visually.

Forcing visual relationships between objects

Another method for enhancing reality is to "similarize" proportions of different objects. By attributing a similar feature to multiple images, you force a relationship between those images. These simple object-to-object resemblances can unify your work, yet they require little time and effort.

For example, if you create a graphic in which two persons share an enlarged or unusual feature, your viewer will assume that they have something more in common as well.

Objects that share identical features are generally assumed to share something else as well.

The woman and man in this graphic are each wearing a fake nose, glasses, and mustache. You may also notice they are holding similar drinks. These affinities draw a viewer into the graphic. Do these two know each other? Will they ever meet? They seem to have so much in common!

Forcing relationships between elements sparks an audience's interest in a graphic. Similar proportions pose questions about a drawing, perhaps inspiring a viewer to inspect your work further or read accompanying text.

When creating any object in a graphic, consider its proportional relationships. Perhaps some features should be scaled within various objects to represent reality more accurately, to enhance reality, or to unify multiple elements in your graphic.

The remaining three building blocks—depth, volume, and color—represent the most advanced methods of drawing theory. Adequate graphics may be produced without any knowledge of these methods. However, by understanding them, you will gain insight into creating sophisticated, expertly crafted illustrations in an electronic environment.

Demonstrating depth

Whether you are drawing with a pencil on a sheet of paper or with a drawing application, you can work with only two dimensions: height and width. How do you create depth? Everything looks flat. How do you draw a road stretching off into nowhere? Or an expansive mountain range? Or even a simple three-dimensional box?

The answer is *perspective*. As explained in the next few pages, you may use perspective to show depth in a drawing, to give an illustration an intensely realistic quality. Since everything you see in the real world has height, width, and depth, your most accurate representations must demonstrate all three of these attributes as well.

Use perspective to demonstrate all three dimensions— height, width, and depth.

Understanding perspective

Perspective is a method used to imitate a third dimension. It can breathe life into a lackluster illustration by adding depth. While not a simple method, it can be mastered with a little effort. We will begin by demonstrating a very simple use of perspective to create a three-dimensional box. Captions under each of the following figures outline the steps in creating our box; the text below the captions explains how each step works and why.

The horizon is a reference line that determines how every portion of a shape is drawn using perspective.

First, draw a straight horizontal line. This will act as the horizon.

The horizon is the line at which the earth meets the sky. It is also the middle of your field of vision. As an object gets farther and farther away, just before it becomes invisible, it will become a speck on the horizon. Suppose you're watching a plane fly away from you. The farther away it flies, the smaller it becomes, and the smaller the distance between it and the horizon line becomes. The plane seems not only to shrink, but also to fly closer and closer to the ground. Prior to disappearing entirely from view, the plane becomes a speck that seems to touch the horizon.

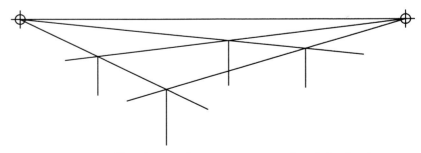

Draw two small sight marks at opposite ends of the horizon. These will act as reference points. Don't worry about the exact location of your reference points, as long as they are

spaced far apart. From each reference point, draw two angled lines, for a total of four lines. Each line from one reference point should cross both lines from the other reference point, as indicated by the four numbered vertical lines.

If you are facing north and a plane flies overhead going due northeast, it will disappear into some point on the right half of the horizon. Likewise, if the plane is going due northwest, it will disappear into some point on the left half of the horizon. These are our reference points. Each reference point indicates the exact point at which the object that we are drawing would disappear if it moved a great distance in the direction of its width or in the direction of its depth.

Take the example of a box. A box has six sides. One side faces up and one faces down. The other four are oriented vertically and face in different compass directions. Suppose we position our box so its four vertical sides are facing due north, east, south, and west. We then look at our box so that we face northeast. Because we face northeast, the reference points for our box represent due north and due east. If our box were to move north (in the direction of its width), it would disappear into the left reference point. If our box were to move east (in the direction of its depth), it would disappear into the right reference point.

In the next example, we'll see how our four angled lines from the last figure represent the top of our box.

A box, or cube, always has six sides: a top, a bottom, and four vertical sides.

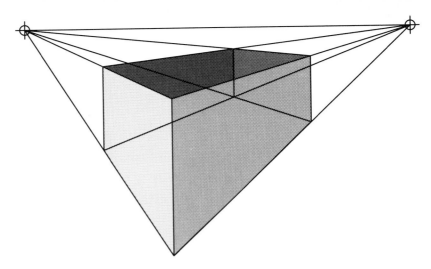

When drawing a cube in perspective, all vertical sides shrink toward a reference point.

Draw four long, vertical lines, one from each point where two angled lines intersect. These represent the corners of the vertical sides of our box. To create the bottom of the box, draw a point somewhere low on the vertical line that appears to be closest to you. From that point, draw a straight line to the left reference point and another to the right reference point. These are the outer sides of the bottom of the box.

We filled in the vertical sides of our box in the previous figure to better display how the final box will look. You can also see how each of the four vertical sides disappears toward one reference point or the other. Our box appears to be jutting out toward the viewer, having depth.

Any cubical object can be drawn in perspective using the method we have described in the previous pages. If you want to practice drawing different boxes, try moving your reference points to different locations on the horizon. Generally, the best perspective drawings have reference points that are as far apart from each other as possible. You may also experiment with adjusting the point on the foremost vertical line that we used to create the bottom of the box. The farther down you move this point, the more dramatic your perspective drawing will be.

Developing a Successful Drawing Technique

You may also develop more complex objects in perspective by setting them inside your perspective cube. The cube helps define the boundaries of the object. All details of your object should be created by drawing lines to your reference points.

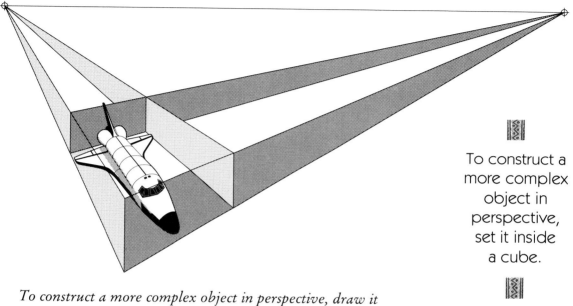

To construct a more complex object in perspective, draw it inside a perspective cube. The cube acts as a set of boundaries and references, and should be erased after your image is completed.

The three-dimensional cube is the most basic of perspective experiments. Understanding the use of the horizon line and its reference points is the first step in learning how to represent depth. But perspective can be a difficult topic, so we'll expand on it. In the following discussion, we will use perspective to create an entire graphic that actually seems to disappear into the horizon.

Extending an object into the horizon

Suppose we wish to draw a long passenger train coming toward us. You may recall that in the *Scaling multiple objects* section of this chapter, we discussed how foreground objects are scaled large and background objects are scaled small. Therefore, the engine of our train will appear as the largest of the cars and the caboose will appear as the smallest. In the following example, the caboose is going to be so far away that we can barely see it. We will create a train that extends backward into oblivion.

A façade that has no depth of its own may remain constant, regardless of the perspective applied to the rest of the object.

We begin by creating the façade, or face, of our engine.

The façade of an image is like the façade of a building; it has no real depth of its own. It is simply the front of the object that we expose to the audience at all times, much like a mask. This allows us to use the same façade repeatedly while experimenting with multiple perspective versions of the rest of the object. Whether viewed from above or below, the façade is an easily identifiable element that always appears the same, thus saving us a great deal of time while testing out different angles of depth.

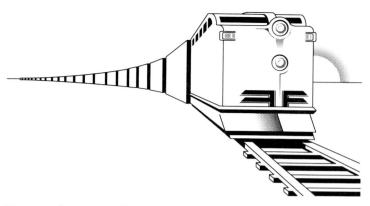

By raising and lowering the horizon, we apply different angles of perspective to the train with out altering its façade.

Here we have attached our façade to a series of very simple boxlike cars. The farther a car is from the engine, the smaller it is scaled. The train track is drawn in perspective, as is the side of the engine. We have also added a sun to highlight our illustration and serve as a reference.

Notice the location of the horizon. It is even with the middle of the train. Since the horizon indicates eye level, we as the viewer are watching the train go by from a normal standing position. The middle of the train is even with the viewer's head. The tracks are at the viewer's feet; the top of the train rises above the viewer.

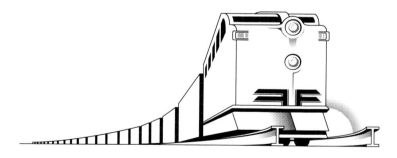

Now we attach our same façade to a different set of cars. We have lowered the horizon so drastically that the viewer's eyes are even with the ground. Since our horizon is lower, all perspective lines are drawn from the base of the graphic.

In the previous figure, we seem to be almost lying on the tracks. Even the rails of the track are taller than we are. This is what is known as a "worm's eye view."

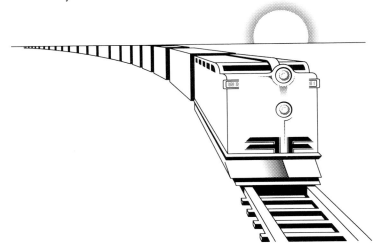

Perspective is a means for representing the location of the viewer in your graphic.

By raising our horizon, we have changed our viewpoint. Notice that despite all the perspective adjustments, our façade remains unchanged.

In the figure above, the entire train is below us. The sun itself seems to be under our lofty gaze. This is called a "bird's eye view."

All of these train drawings are impressive, despite the fact that they were simple to create. The only detailed part of our drawing—the façade—remains constant regardless of the elevation of the horizon. All portions of the figures that are subjected to perspective are simple in structure and design—just a row of boxes! The effect is elegant; the approach is minimalist and requires little ability or time.

Perspective is a means for representing the location of the viewer in your graphic, thus drawing an audience into your picture. Use perspective when you want to create a realistic graphic environment that will warm viewers to your concept.

The next few pages explain two more methods for demonstrating depth that are easier to implement than perspective.

Developing a Successful Drawing Technique

High detail and low focus

Focus is one of the methods for indicating depth that may be used instead of or in addition to perspective. Like a camera lens, the human eye can focus clearly on only one object at a time. Hold your finger close to your face and examine it. Now notice with your peripheral vision how objects behind your finger are out of focus. This is the effect you want to imitate in your graphics.

When you draw an object that seems to be close to the viewer, bring out as many details as possible. Show very small features that you notice only upon intense examination. If something is farther away, ten to twenty feet, draw it normally, showing only those details that are necessary to your concept. If an object is far from the viewer, ignore details, indicating its basic form and the minimum information needed to clarify its identity.

Draw close objects in high detail; draw distant objects out of focus.

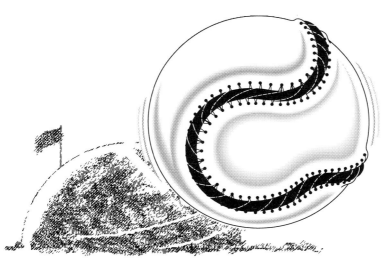

Here are two circular objects, both equal in size. However, the baseball is far forward of the domed stadium. In fact, the baseball is so close that we can see every thread that secures the cover to its core. The dome is obviously far away because it is out of focus.

Another way to indicate that an object is far away is to draw a haze in front of it, as if it is obscured by ground heat, smoke, fog, pollution, or clouds. After all, if you can see clouds in front of an image, it must be miles from where you are.

When drawing a nearby object, represent as much detail as possible. If the object is far away, draw only the basic form of the object and enough detail to make it recognizable. And if it's somewhere between, draw the object as you would normally, indicating accurate form, scale, and proportion. Focus gives your graphics an extra sense of depth and reality that your viewer will appreciate.

The third method for indicating depth is the easiest. This method simply requires that you fill objects with lightening or darkening shades of gray.

Shades of depth

Our final method for indicating depth makes use of shades of gray. This technique is used primarily to represent depth among a group of distant objects. When a group of objects is far away, the closest of the objects should be darkest, the farthest of the objects should be lightest.

The best example is a mountain range. The entire range may be miles away. To effectively add depth and realism to your drawing, you want to indicate that some mountains in the range are closer than others. The most distant mountain is the lightest, the second-to-farthest is darker, the third-to-farthest is a little darker yet, and so on, until you arrive at the closest mountain, which should be almost completely black. No detail or focus is required, nor is any perspective. You simply fill each element with a gray value or color to achieve the effect of distance.

When a group of objects is far away, the closest of them is the darkest, the most distant is the lightest.

If you want to
awe your
viewers, add
depth to your
drawing.

*The first mountain in our range is almost black. As the
towers recede, the shades of gray lighten. The farthest
mountain is the lightest shade of all.*

Whenever you draw a mountain range or other far-away group
of objects, use different shades of a color to indicate depth. This is
one of the simplest techniques in this book, yet—like most simple
techniques—its effect is dramatic and appealing.

———————————◆●◆———————————

Depth transforms your graphics from flat representations into
pictorial environments. Adding depth to your drawing using perspective, focus, and simple shading can add sophisticated realism to the
most modest graphic.

The next building block of drawing theory is volume, which can
be used to demonstrate depth within a single object.

Representing volume

Perspective is a method for displaying objects in relation to their distance from the viewer. By contrast, *volume* adds depth to a single object.

For example, a globe of the world has volume. One point is always closer to us than any other point on the surface of the globe. If we are looking at the ridges of the Swiss Alps, then Switzerland is closer to us than Canada, Brazil, Ethiopia, or Japan. If we spin the globe, some new country will loom toward us as Switzerland fades away.

Many other objects, such as cups, vases, lamps, tennis balls, and wheels, have volume as well. Even things that aren't round, like pencils, books, telephones, bricks, and radios, have volume.

To demonstrate volume, you must have a source of light to bring out subtle and dramatic shading differences. By using highlights and shadows, as we will discuss in the next few pages, you can give your drawings an added sense of dimension.

By using highlights and shadows, you give your drawings an added sense of dimension.

Understanding origin of light

Light is the most important element in rendering volume. After sketching the objects in your drawing, begin indicating volume by determining an origin of light—such as the sun or a lamp—that will be constant from object to object. All highlights and shadows will be based on this light source. A light source need not be displayed in your drawing. It may be implied, provided that the lighting is consistent from object to object.

The origin of light determines the size and position of highlights and shadows. Highlights appear at places where light is reflected off an object. Shadows appear where light is unable to reach regions that

Developing a Successful Drawing Technique

are blocked by the object itself. Another way to think of the light source is this: If you were the light source, highlights would be the portions of an object that you can see and shadows would be the portions that you can't see.

The following examples demonstrate how to draw a voluminous sphere using an origin of light to determine the position of highlights and to project shadows.

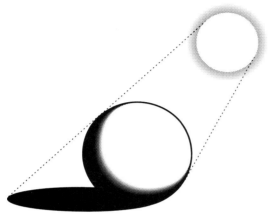

Portions of an object that are touched by light are highlighted, those that are not touched by light dwell in shadow.

In the figure above, we have drawn a sun and a sphere. The sun acts as our light source. By drawing two sight lines from the sides of our sun to the sides of the sphere, we can determine how light is reflected and where light cannot reach.

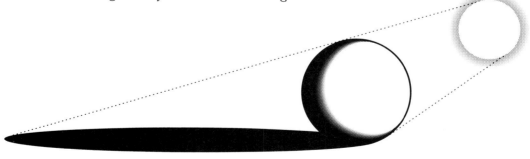

As we move the light source or the object, shadows and highlights change. Here we have moved our sun down and to the right. The angles of our sight lines have also changed, as shown by a lengthened shadow and a rotated highlight.

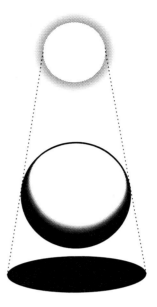

Now we have moved not only the sun, but the sphere as well. The sphere hovers above the ground, so that its shadow is no longer connected to it. The shadow is also shorter. Shadows are always smallest when the light source is located directly above an object.

Ground shadows can be used to indicate the nature of an object's environment.

In each of our figures, we have drawn sight lines that determine where shadows should begin and end. Also notice in each figure that we have drawn a shadow not only on the sphere itself, but also on the ground below. This is a simplified method for indicating the nature of an object's environment—whether the ground is flat or bumpy or jagged—without actually drawing a background, detail for detail.

Light demonstrates the volume of an object. Portions of an object that are touched by the light are highlighted; portions that are not touched are shadowed. Shadows can also be used to infer a background without drawing it in detail. Contrasts between dark and light indicate the volume of an image and add authenticity to your representation.

Developing a Successful Drawing Technique

The next example demonstrates how to add shade and gradations to an object in order to indicate a complex volume.

Shading and gradation

Creating highlights and shadows often involves more work than our sphere example might lead you to believe. Many objects have surface details that are best rendered with shading and gradation. A gradation is the gradual passing from one shade of a color to another. For example, suppose that you scribble on some paper with a piece of soft charcoal. If you rub at the scribble with your finger, you smear the transition between the black of the charcoal and the white of the paper, creating a gradation. Gradations can also be achieved in a drawing program.

To demonstrate the use of gradation, we will create a voluminous object in four steps. The following examples begin with the construction of a vase and take us through the definition of its light source and shading.

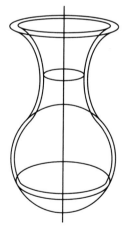

It is often useful to create an accurate sketch using only geometric shapes.

We construct our vase as the combination of many circles and ovals. The line through the center demonstrates our initial regard for symmetry. Every curved line on the left of the vase is repeated in mirror image on the right.

It is often useful to develop an object geometrically. Try creating a sketch relying heavily on your program's rectangle and oval tools. This provides you with an exacting base form; later you may build upon this vase in a less rigid style.

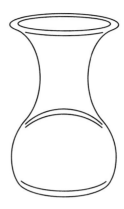

We delete the extraneous sketch lines to produce this crisp line drawing of the vase. The form is elegant, but so far we have no indication of volume.

An even gradation can be used as a sketch for more complex shading.

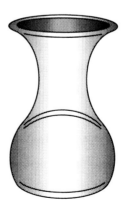

Next, we create two symmetrical gradations—one from dark to light and one from light to dark—inside the body of the vase. Inside the mouth of the vase, we darken the gradations. The addition of symmetrical gradations does not add volume, but is a first step toward this.

Notice that our first figure was a sketch of the form of the vase. The last gradation is a sketch of the vase's volume. Though we have yet to determine an origin of light or create any naturalistic shading, we have provided an excellent starting point.

Finally, we add shading based upon a light source that is directly above the vase. Notice that the bottom of the vase is highlighted much like our earlier sphere, demonstrating its round form. We have also added arms to make the vase more interesting.

Determining a light source and sketching a gradation are the first two steps in demonstrating the volume of an object. Modifying the gradation to include additional highlights and shadows completes the realistic effect.

Shading is a difficult technique to learn in a theoretical context. Understanding how to use shading and gradations is one aspect, but actually creating shading and gradations in a drawing program is a separate issue. To learn how to create a gradation, refer to the *Creating seamless gradations* section of Chapter 4. In addition, you may try out the sample project in Chapter 7, which demonstrates a step-by-step procedure for drawing a voluminous lamp.

Our image of the vase demonstrates how shading may be applied to a gradated sketch to indicate a light source. It also features the qualities of reflection and reflected light. Both qualities, which are explained in the following paragraphs, add elegance to our graphic.

Reflection and reflected light

Notice the shading underneath the vase in the previous figure. It begins as a nondescript shadow, then develops into a mirror image of the vase itself. This shows that the surface upon which the vase rests is shiny, or reflective. Perhaps it is a well waxed table or glazed porcelain countertop. In any case, by creating a vague mirror image of the vase, we have not only demonstrated light and volume, we have also defined the background of our graphic. We imply the nature of the ground without drawing the ground itself.

Notice the shading in the body of the vase. The circular white area in the center of the bottom portion of the vase is surrounded by degrees of shading that fade from white to dark gray, and then to a medium gray. Rather than getting progressively darker, our shading gets dark, and then lightens. Why is this? How can shadows become lighter as they recede from the light source?

There is, in fact, a second light source. Since our table top is shiny enough to reflect the vase, it also reflects light from our source. This reflected light is dimmed, but it is sufficient to shed a highlight along what would otherwise be the darkest perimeter of the vase.

Reflection and reflected light allow you to convey your background in a discreet and time-saving manner.

Use reflection and reflected light to imply an object's environment without displaying the background in full detail. These techniques are fairly advanced, but once mastered they save a great deal of time and add luster and elegance to your work.

By correctly displaying the qualities of volume, you demonstrate your knowledge of complex drawing theory.

Almost every object in real life has volume. By displaying highlights, shadows, gradations, and reflections, you show your viewer that you understand the appearance of your image and its environment. This also demonstrates your knowledge of complex drawing theory and makes graphics very impressive.

Always consider your source of light in a drawing and keep it consistent from object to object. Concentrate on where light touches an object, and what portions of an object are in darkness.

Our final building block involves the creation of color graphics.

Adding color

Most Macintosh users own monochrome monitors—monitors that show only black and white. This is particularly true for people with a Mac SE or older model computer. However, if you own a Mac II series model with a color monitor and an 8-bit video card or better, you can take advantage of between 256 colors and 6 million colors. Even so, most electronically produced drawings, including retail clip-art, are created in black and white or gray scale. Because color printing is expensive, and the quality of color separations currently varies among software and output devices, color drawings are uncommon outside the realm of glossy, professional publications. (With the exception of the cover, for example, no color drawings appear in this book.)

For most purposes, a black-and-white graphic is sufficient. But if you own or have access to compatible hardware and software (see Chapter 10), you may want to add color to your drawings. The following discussion of basic color theory is designed to help you select and use colors and shades of colors.

Understanding color models

Whether they appear on a computer screen or in a magazine ad, all hues (subtle variations in color) can be created by mixing two or more primary colors. The identity of these primary colors depends on the *color model* being used:

1. The *RGB* (red, green, blue), or *additive primary model*. This is the color model used by your monitor and other projection devices such as your TV set. Red, green, and blue light is projected from your monitor in a variety of intensities to produce desired colors. (The term "additive" refers to the fact that the more primary color you add, the lighter the resulting color becomes.)

In the RGB color model:

A. Equal intensities of red and green light make yellow. Subtract some red light to produce chartreuse; subtract some green light to produce orange.

B. Equal intensities of green and blue light make cyan. Subtract some green light to produce turquoise; subtract some blue light to produce jade.

C. Equal intensities of blue and red light make purple. Subtract some blue light to produce magenta; subtract some red light to produce violet.

D. Equal intensities of red, green, and blue make white or gray.

E. No light results in black (or darkness).

2. The *CMYK* (cyan, magenta, yellow, black), or *subtractive primary model.* This is the color model used when printing in color. Cyan, magenta, yellow, and black pigments are applied to white paper in a variety of intensities to produce desired colors. (The term "subtractive" refers to the fact that the more primary color you add, the darker the resulting color becomes.)

In the CMYB color model:

A. Equal amounts of cyan and magenta pigments make violet. Add some cyan pigmentation to produce blue; add some magenta pigmentation to produce purple.

B. Equal amounts of magenta and yellow pigments make red. Add some magenta pigmentation to produce carmine; add some yellow pigmentation to produce orange.

C. Equal amounts of yellow and cyan pigments make green. Add some yellow pigmentation to produce chartreuse; add some cyan pigmentation to produce turquoise.

D. Equal amounts of cyan, magenta, and yellow pigments make brown.

E. Add black pigmentation to any other pigment to darken the color.

F. No pigmentation results in white (the color of the paper).

These models are important to remember when mixing color on screen and when printing.

Color models determine how color is displayed on your monitor or printed on a page.

Printing in color

If you or your company owns a color laser printer or color dot-matrix printer, you may print small quantities of color graphics. You may also use color printers to print *composites*, which help you determine what your final graphic will look like when printed commercially.

If you do not have access to a color printer, the only way to create printed color graphics is through a commercial printer. This is an expensive process, usually requiring a run of more than a thousand copies to make the process cost-effective.

There are two methods of commercial color printing:

Always consult your commercial printer prior to creating any final output of your graphic.

1. *Spot color printing* is the cheaper of the two methods if you plan on using black and only one or two other colors. Spot colors are generally premixed according to the Pantone Matching System, which defines several hundred colors and offers a catalog display of these colors. Many drawing programs also support Pantone colors, so that you can emulate your finished artwork on screen.

2. *Process color printing* is more expensive but allows you to create every color in the spectrum using the CMYK or subtractive primary model. When printing to your laser printer, the drawing software separates your graphic into four prints, representing the cyan, magenta, yellow, and black primary components of every color in the graphic. You then submit these sheets to your commercial printer. The commercial printer in turn produces multiple copies of your graphic by applying cyan ink per your cyan separation, magenta ink per your magenta separation, and so on.

Whether you intend to use the spot color or process color printing method, you should consult your commercial printer prior to creating any final output of your graphic. You will want to ensure that the colors you see on your monitor closely match the colors produced by your commercial printer, since your monitor and your commercial

Developing a Successful Drawing Technique

printer use different color models. It is also a good idea to make sure that you can provide color composites with your separations. Miscommunication can lead to increased costs for last-minute paste-up and other problems.

Most importantly, give yourself plenty of time. Consult with your printer to determine how much time your job will require. If you allow the printer less than the standard number of days to complete your job, plan on increased printing costs due to rush charges.

Using like and contrasting colors

If you intend to use a wide variety of colors in a single graphic, whether for on-screen presentational work or for process color printing, you should know how to use different colors to produce harmonious effects. Basically, two colors placed side by side will produce one of three results:

Whenever you draw in color, consider how colors appear when positioned next to one another.

1. If the two colors are a *like pair*, they will blend into each other. Examples of like pairs are purple and violet, blue and cyan, green and emerald, pale ochre and lemon yellow, red and scarlet, brown and siena, and black and gray. Like colors are often used to produce gradation effects.

2. If the two colors are a *contrasting pair*, they will produce a fluorescence at the point where they meet, as if the colors are bouncing off each other. Examples of contrasting pairs are deep red and bright green, orange and blue, and lemon yellow and violet.

3. If the two colors are neither like nor contrasting, there are no specific implications. Thus they are called a *neutral pair*. This describes the majority of color pairs: gray and red, orange and turquoise, violet and emerald, and many, many more.

In general, you can use like pairs and neutral pairs freely. Contrasting pairs, however, should be used sparingly. Contrasting pairs, like dissonant chords in music, can produce unpleasant results if used unwisely.

Whenever you draw in color, consider how colors appear when positioned next to one another. If the colors are like colors, they can flow together to produce shading effects, as discussed in the following paragraphs. If neighboring colors are neutral, your graphic will have a conservative appearance. Juxtaposing contrasting colors is a bold gesture, that can produce dramatic effects if used with care. By carefully considering your use of neighboring colors, you ensure a tasteful and elegant graphic.

Color shading

The last topic in this chapter is color shading. Like black and white shading, color shading involves using progressively lighter or darker shades of a base color. You may create a lighter version of a color by decreasing its tint. Tint is measured in terms of percentage. Therefore, a 50% tint of red is half as dark as a solid (100%) red. As you might guess, a 90% tint of a color and an untinted version of the same color would be considered a like pair.

You can create full color graphics that will impress audiences as no black and white drawings can.

 Darkening a color is more difficult. Typically, the beginning artist will create a darker shade of a color by adding black to it. While not entirely unacceptable, this is not the best solution. Often, adding black to a color, especially to yellow, will produce muddy, unattractive results. The best solution is to darken the color by adding its contrasting pair partner. For example, if you wanted to produce a darker shade of blue, add some orange; for a darker shade of red, add green; for a darker yellow, add purple, and vice versa. Darkening by this method produces natural shades that mix well.

However, how this color theory applies to your specific drawing application will vary. Most programs use RGB color mixing models; some also offer CMYK, and some even allow you to mix two existing colors on screen. But regardless of your color model, when shading a colored object, use tints to produce highlights and use mixes containing contrasting colors to produce shadows. The result will be an attractive, gradual transition from color to like color.

Keep in mind that drawing in color is most useful if you have access to a Macintosh II with a color monitor. If you have a monochrome system, you can still create color artwork, but you must plan your choices more carefully. You may also need a color output device or a high-quality monochrome laser printer if you intend to create color separations for a commercial printer. However expensive color graphics may be to produce, the use of color can lead to magnificent results when used correctly. By understanding color models and effectively utilizing neighboring colors and color shading, you can create masterful color drawings that will far surpass the impact of black-and-white graphics.

The Drawing Environment

As you may have already noticed, drawing applications make up a large portion of the personal computer software market. Many brands of drawing software exist, and they vary substantially in both price and sophistication. While methods of operation may also vary widely from program to program, most drawing applications share several features that constitute the basic drawing environment. We will discuss these fundamental similarities throughout this chapter.

Depending on your brand of software, you may occasionally encounter an operation that does not work according to our description. We have designed this chapter to make these occurrences as infrequent as possible. If we describe a feature that seems to be missing from your application, you may refer to the product listing in Chapter 10 to confirm the areas in which your software is lacking or to discover how a specific feature works differently in your software.

Terminology

Throughout this chapter and the remainder of this book, we will refer to two primary mouse operations. The first, *clicking*, means to press your mouse button and immediately release. The second, *dragging*, means to press your mouse button, move your mouse to a new location, and release the button. Other actions are based on these two operations. For example, to *double-click* is to press and release your mouse button twice in rapid succession.

The term "mouse" is used as a generic reference to any point device, including joy sticks, track balls, or tablets.

Incidentally, we use the term "mouse" as a generic reference to any pointing device, including not only the standard single-button mouse, but also any joystick, trackball, tablet, or light pen.

To draw with any drawing application, you must choose commands and operate tools. Choose a command by pressing your mouse button on the appropriate menu bar and then dragging down to or clicking on the command name in the list displayed. Generally, choosing a command produces some kind of alteration to a specified element. A tool, on the other hand, is selected by clicking its icon in your application's toolbox. You then use the selected tool in your program's drawing window to create and manipulate the elements that make up your graphic.

Each icon shown in this chapter is a generic enlargement of a similar drawing tool. These icons are intended as a graphical means of introducing features provided by most applications. If your software does not offer a tool that matches our icon, it may simply be that your tool has a different appearance. Alternatively, the feature may be available in a different form, such as a command or a mouse operation. We will try to account for such application variations in our text.

Finally, this chapter does not discuss all features available in a typical drawing program. For example, we make no mention of scroll bars, rulers, view sizes, status bars, and other features not directly related to the creation and manipulation of lines and shapes.

The rest of this chapter describes how to use features in a typical drawing program.

Our tool icons are a graphic means of introducing features provided by most drawing applications.

Geometric lines and shapes

Most drawing programs provide one or more line tools and a variety of shape tools that are useful for creating geometric forms.

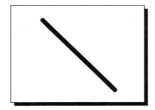

The line tool is used to draw straight lines at any angle.

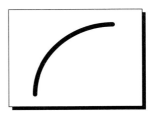

The arc tool is used to create a curved line that forms a quarter ellipse (or oval).

Using the geometric shape tools, you can create rectangles, squares, rectangles with rounded corners, circles, and ellipses.

The following pages discuss how each of these tools is used to create simple geometric objects.

Creating simple lines

You may constrain the angle of a line to a multiple of 45° by pressing the shift key.

The line tool is an easy tool to operate. Simply press your mouse button and drag with the line tool to create a straight line. The line begins when you click and ends when you release. Therefore, the angle of the line is determined by the angle of your drag. If you drag horizontally, you create a horizontal line. If you drag diagonally, you create a diagonal line.

You may also *constrain* the angle of a line to a multiple of 45° by pressing the shift key.

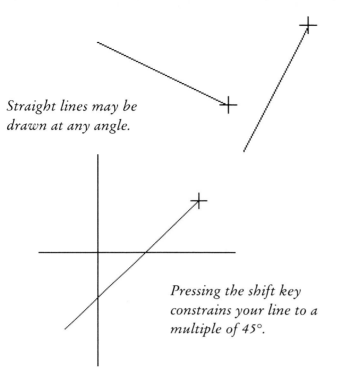

Straight lines may be drawn at any angle.

Pressing the shift key constrains your line to a multiple of 45°.

Drawing with the arc tool is equally simple. As you drag, however, your line bends to form a quarter ellipse, as shown below. Press the shift key to constrain the arc to a quarter circle.

Use the arc tool to create a quarter ellipse or quarter circle between two points.

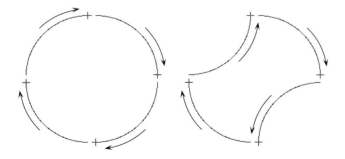

Drag with the arc tool to create a curved line between two points. In some applications, the arc always progresses clockwise, as shown on the left. In others, it begins from a top or bottom point and ends at a side point, as shown on the right.

Not all applications provide line tools. If yours does not, you may easily create both straight and curved lines using the pen tool, as discussed in the next section, *Free-form lines and shapes*.

Creating simple shapes

Drawing geometric shapes such as rectangles and ovals is as easy as drawing a line.

Creating a shape is a simple matter of dragging with one of the three shape tools.

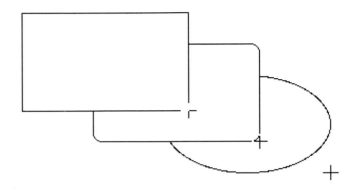

These three examples demonstrate the results of dragging with the rectangle tool, the rounded rectangle tool, and the oval tool. To operate each tool, you create the shape from any corner to its opposite corner. Most programs also provide an option that allows you to create a simple shape from center to corner, so that the beginning of your drag is the center of the shape.

If you press the shift key while drawing with the rectangle or rounded rectangle tool, you constrain your shape to a square. If you press the shift key while drawing with the oval tool, you create a circle.

Developing a Successful Drawing Technique

Use a line or shape tool when you want to quickly create a geometric object. We will examine how to manipulate lines and shapes created with these tools later in this chapter.

Free-form lines and shapes

The freehand, polygon, and Bézier curve tools allow you to draw free-form lines and shapes to the most complex specifications.

The freehand tool allows you to quickly and easily draw free-form objects.

The polygon and Bézier curve tools provide meticulous control when drawing complex, free-form shapes.

The polygon and Bézier curve tools are more time-consuming to operate, but give you more meticulous control over your drawings.

The following pages discuss how each of these tools is used to create objects of any shape and size imaginable.

Drawing freehand paths

When you draw with a pencil on a piece of paper, you press the lead against the page and draw. You use the same method to operate the freehand tool in a drawing program. Pressing your mouse button and dragging creates a line that follows the course of your cursor movements. Such a line is often called a *path*.

Even if you are experienced with drawing on paper, you may at first find it difficult to create clean, consistent lines in your drawing program. This skill is primarily a matter of practice. Since a computer mouse is bulkier than a pencil, it may seem awkward and unfamiliar initially, but will become more familiar as you continue to use it. And the more familiar you are with moving your mouse, the better you will use the freehand tool.

To greatly improve the appearance of your paths, try drawing very slowly. Especially when learning to draw with a mouse, your accuracy will increase as your speed decreases.

A free-form line or shape created in a drawing program is called a path.

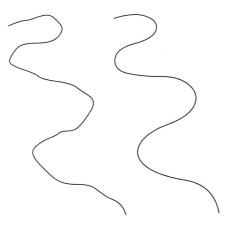

The path on the left was created by drawing quickly with the freehand tool. This line has many irregularities, which give the path a sloppy, imprecise appearance. The path on the right was drawn more slowly and carefully. It appears more even, smooth, and professional.

Some programs also allow you to control the sensitivity of the freehand tool. When you first begin to use this tool, you will probably want to decrease, or loosen, the tool's sensitivity, in order to allow the drawing program to ignore minor inconsistencies in your cursor movements. As your mouse control becomes more precise, you may incrementally tighten the tool's sensitivity to track your movements more exactly.

Don't worry if your freehand images don't look exactly right on your first attempt. You can always edit a free-form line or shape, as we will explain in the *Reshaping paths* section of this chapter.

The freehand tool is great for creating free-form paths quickly and approximately. But no matter how adept you become at using your mouse, most of your freehand images will require adjustments and alterations. If you're willing to spend a little extra time and effort, you can draw your paths correctly the first time using your program's polygon or Bézier curve tool.

Drawing paths point by point

All drawing programs offer some kind of tool that allows you to create an object as a series of individual points. In some programs this tool is the polygon tool. To operate the tool, click to establish the first corner point in a path. Then move your mouse and click at additional points to create additional corners. As you click, each corner point is connected to the previous point by a straight *segment*. To finish the object, close the shape by clicking on your first corner point, or double-click to allow the polygon to remain open.

Use the polygon or Bézier curve tool to create corner points joined by straight segments.

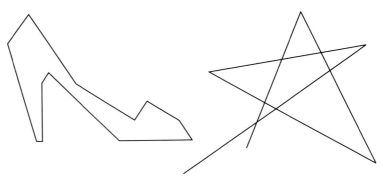

In the shape on the left, we closed the polygon by clicking on the first point in the shape. To create the open line on the right, we ended the polygon by double-clicking.

After completing a polygon, you may leave the path as it is, with straight sides, or you may choose a "Smooth" command to round off the edges, creating an object that looks like it was drawn with the freehand tool. Straight segments no longer connect corner points rigidly; instead, segments curve toward points without ever quite touching them.

Choose the "Smooth" command to round off the edges in a straight-sided path.

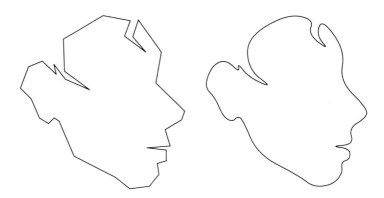

We first created the outline of a face with the polygon tool to exactly position the corner points in the path. We then chose the "Smooth" command to round out the segments and make the face appear more naturalistic.

Unfortunately, the "Smooth" command rounds out all segments in a shape and eliminates all corners. If you want a couple curved segments to meet in a crisp corner, you must position one point directly in front of another.

To create a corner in a smoothed path, overlap one point onto its neighbor.

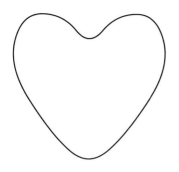

In the first shape, only one point exists at each of the cusps in the valentine. As a result, the path is curving rather than forming crisp corners at these cusps. To create a corner at each cusp, we create a second point and overlap it onto its neighbor, as shown in the second valentine.

The polygon tool allows you to precisely position points in a shape, but it doesn't provide much control over the manner in which individual segments curve. Although points in a smoothed polygon guide curves like invisible hands pulling at a piece of rubber wire, no segment is ever anchored. Adjusting a single point can upset every segment in the path.

A more precise tool for creating free-form lines and shapes is the Bézier curve tool. Using this tool, you first anchor a segment and then bend the segment with respect to the anchor point.

Drawing paths with Bézier curves

A few drawing applications do not offer a Bézier curve tool, which is unfortunate, since this tool provides precise control over freehand shapes. With this tool, you can combine corner points with smooth segments and control the exact curvature of a segment. If your program does not offer a Bézier curve tool, you will have to rely on smooth polygons, as we have described on the previous page.

In many ways, you may think of the Bézier curve tool as a "souped-up" polygon tool. If you simply click with the tool, you will create corner points, just as if you had used a polygon tool. However, if you drag with the tool, you create a smooth point that has two *Bézier control handles*. These handles act as levers, bending segments relative to the smooth point itself.

Dragging with the Bézier curve tool creates a smooth point flanked by two Bézier control handles.

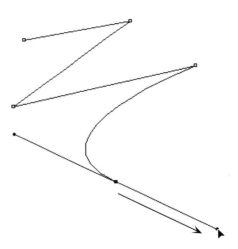

Clicking with a Bézier curve tool creates corner points, as demonstrated by the first four points in our path. If you click and drag, the point at which you click becomes a smooth point and the location at which you release becomes a Bézier control handle. This handle will affect the next segment you create. A second control handle appears symmetrically about the smooth point to the first. This handle determines the curve of the most recent segment, as shown above.

Developing a Successful Drawing Technique

The Bézier control handles on either side of a smooth point are locked into alignment with each other. This ensures that a line curves evenly as it passes through the smooth point. To make two curved segments meet in a corner point, you must be able to move each Bézier control handle independently. Different programs allow you to do this in different ways. In a program like Aldus FreeHand, you break the alignment between the two handles by pressing the option key while creating a smooth point. In Adobe Illustrator, you first create a smooth point, then change it to a corner point by dragging on the point again while pressing the option key.

Independent Bézier control handles allow you to draw curved segments that meet to form a cusp.

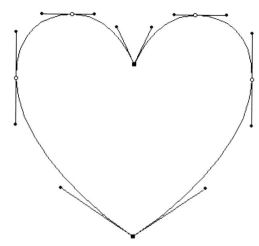

We have redrawn our valentine shape, this time using the Bézier curve tool. All points and their control handles are displayed. The pair of control handles associated with any of the four smooth points (displayed as hollow) are locked into alignment with each other. But the control handles associated with the two corner points (displayed as black) are independent, allowing us to create cusps at these points.

Notice our most recent valentine includes uniform curves. By comparison, the heart from the smoothed polygon figure appears rather squished, almost dented in places. While the difference may seem very slight, these kinds of subtleties can add up to improve or impair the quality of a complex drawing. In pure drawing terms, the Bézier curve tool is the most valuable feature any drawing application has to offer.

The trace tool automatically converts scanned art and sketches into free-form paths.

To summarize, use the freehand tool when you want to quickly draw a free-form path without having to worry about positioning points or Bézier control handles. The results may be rough, but you can always adjust the shape as described in the *Reshaping paths* section later in this chapter.

To create complex paths correctly the first time, skilled users will prefer to use a point-by-point tool such as the polygon or Bézier curve tool. Although you may apply a "Smooth" command to paths drawn with the polygon tool, this tool does not allow you to anchor curved segments. Using the Bézier curve tool, you may create both the corner points and the smooth points required to anchor segments as well as the control handles required to bend the segments.

A Bézier curve tool is essential for the creation of elegant, free-form drawings. In fact, if your program lacks such a tool, you may want to consider upgrading. For recommendations, see Chapter 10.

Tracing bitmaps

Not everyone can be a Rembrandt. Some of us are lucky to draw a straight line, much less triumph over a complex feature like the Bézier curve tool. Others can draw quite adequately with pencil and paper, but have problems converting their skills to a computer program.

For the non-computer artist, many programs provide a trace tool that automatically traces a bitmapped image with a series of free-form paths.

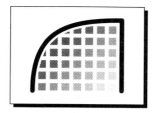

The trace tool converts jagged bitmaps into smooth drawings.

In the next few pages, we will discuss how to automatically trace sketches that have been created in painting programs, scanned artwork, and other bitmapped images. But first, we will look briefly at the difference between a bitmapped painting and an object-oriented drawing. We will also explain the rationale for using bitmaps as a starting point in the drawing process.

Objects and bitmaps

It is not easy to draw from scratch in a drawing program. Even if you draw exclusively with the freehand tool, you must frequently edit your lines and shapes, point by point. Also, drawing programs require you to represent images as a collage of mathematically defined objects. Lines and shapes must be layered on top of one another like girders in a building.

Painting programs provide friendly drawing environments, but produce jagged output.

Because using a drawing program is partially an architectural experience, the best user of drawing software is probably part artist and part engineer. For those of us who aren't engineers, a painting application like MacPaint provides a more artist-friendly environment.

Painting programs provide simple tools such as pencils and erasers. And since little interpretation is required by your software, these tools work just like their real-life counterparts. Your screen displays the results of your mouse movements instantaneously. This allows you to draw, see what you've drawn, and make alterations, all in the time it takes the appropriate neurons to fire in your brain.

But despite the many advantages of painting software, its single failing—the graininess of its output—is glaringly obvious, so much so that people who have never used a computer can immediately recognize a bitmapped image as computer-produced artwork. Object-oriented drawings, on the other hand, are smooth.

By tracing a bit-mapped image, you exploit both a painting program's friendliness and a drawing program's smooth output.

The bitmapped fish on the left was fairly easy to create, but it has the kind of jagged edges many viewers associate with computer art. The object-oriented fish on the right required more time and effort, but the result is smooth and professional-looking.

By tracing a bitmapped image in a drawing program, you can have the best of both worlds. You can sketch your idea traditionally onto a piece of paper and then scan it into your computer, or you can sketch directly in a painting program. Either way, your sketch will be bitmapped. Import the sketch into your drawing program as a tracing template. Then use your program's trace tool to convert the image to free-form paths.

Operating the trace tool

Depending on your program, you typically operate the trace tool in one of two ways. In some programs, you surround the painted image in a marquee. Drag with the text tool from corner to opposite corner around the image you want to trace. As you drag, you create a rectangular, dotted marquee. Upon releasing your mouse button, your drawing program automatically traces all portions of the bitmapped image inside the marquee. If your sketch is fairly complicated, the tracing process may take a few minutes to execute.

In other programs you click the trace tool just outside the perimeter of your sketch. A path is created around the outer edge of the bitmap. You then have to click just inside each of the white areas of the sketch, tracing each one individually. For example, to trace a sketch of the letter "O," you would click once to trace around the outside of the letter and a second time to trace around the inside.

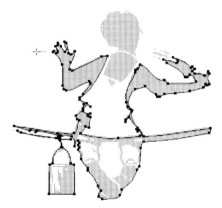

Trace tools provide the best results when your sketch is drawn in black and white with few stray pixels.

In a program like Aldus Freehand, you may surround a bitmap in a marquee with the trace tool (left). This instructs the program to create several paths at once. In Adobe Illustrator, you may only trace one path at a time (right).

Most trace tools produce the most useful results when your sketch is created in black and white with few stray pixels. However, even the best traced images requires some clean-up. Not only do paths require reshaping, they must also be filled with the appropriate colors. After tracing your letter "O," for example, you would have to fill the outer path with black and the inner path with white. You might also have to juggle the layering of the two objects so that the white shape is in front of the black. (For more information about layering, see the *Transforming objects* section later in this chapter.)

Because no trace tool converts a sketch flawlessly, most traced objects must be reshaped.

After tracing the sketch from the previous figure, the image appears as shown on the left. Not only are the shapes filled incorrectly, but some of the details are inaccurate or unclear. The hands have been traced especially unsatisfactorily. A substantial amount of reshaping and redrawing is required to produce the finished image on the right.

As tempting as it may be, do not rely on the trace tool as a panacea for all your drawing woes. While many programs allow you to control the tool's accuracy, no trace tool converts a sketch flawlessly. Most traced objects will have to be reshaped, refined, or redrawn.

When you are creating a complex drawing, we recommend that you first sketch your idea with pencil and paper, since these tools are probably most familiar to you, and then scan the image into your computer. If you don't have access to a scanner, create simple black-and-white sketches in a painting program like MacPaint. You may

Developing a Successful Drawing Technique

then trace your sketch using the freehand or Bézier curve tool, or use the trace tool to instruct your drawing software do the work.

If you use the trace tool, keep in mind that your converted image can be considered only an approximation of the final picture. You will have to spend some time adjusting and fine-tuning your lines and shapes. In the following section, we examine how to reshape paths, from manipulating the curvature of segments to adding, deleting, and moving points.

Regardless of the tool used to create paths, most will need some adjustment.

Reshaping paths

Assuming that you create most of your lines and shapes with the freehand and trace tools, most of your lines and shapes are going to need some adjustments. In many applications, these adjustments may be performed with the standard arrow tool. But other programs require that you use a special tool or command to reshape objects.

In many programs, the standard arrow (or pointer) tool allows you to select and manipulate an existing object.

Other programs provide special reshape tools that allow you to perform many kinds of manipulations.

The following pages describe how these tools are used to reshape both geometric and free-form elements.

Selecting an element

Before you may reshape a path, you must select it. Typically, a path is selected with the arrow tool. In a few programs, such as Adobe Illustrator or Aldus FreeHand, a selected free-form path displays its points so that you can immediately begin reshaping the path. But in most applications, clicking on a geometric or free-form path with the arrow tool displays eight *transformation handles*, which surround the path in a rectangular formation. These handles are commonly used to stretch and rotate an image, as described in the *Transforming objects* section later in this chapter.

To reshape a path, you must first click on it with the arrow tool to select it.

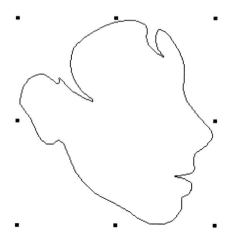

In most drawing applications, a path selected with the arrow tool displays handles that form a rectangle around the image.

After selecting a path with the arrow tool, you may choose a "Reshape" command or the equivalent to display individual points in order to manipulate the form of the path. In most software, this command is available from a standard menu. An exception to this is

Canvas, in which you choose the "Edit Pts" command by pressing the option key and dragging at one of the free-form drawing tool icons.

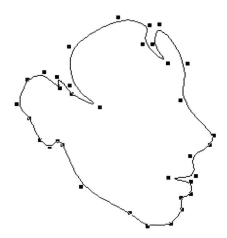

In some programs, you choose a "Reshape" command to display the points in a path.

Choosing the "Reshape" command displays all points in the selected free-form path.

After displaying the points of a free-form path, you may move, add, and delete points, adjust Bézier control handles, and so on. If your selected path was created with one of the geometric tools, however, your options vary, depending on your software.

Reshaping rectangles and ovals

In a more sophisticated program like Adobe Illustrator or Aldus FreeHand, geometric objects such as rectangles and ovals are treated as *grouped* paths. When you group one or more elements (by choosing the "Group" command), you combine all selected points and paths into a single object, locking the relative distances between points so they cannot be altered.

To reshape a grouped geometric object in such a program, simply choose the "Ungroup" command. The shapes become free-form paths whose points may be moved and Bézier control handles adjusted.

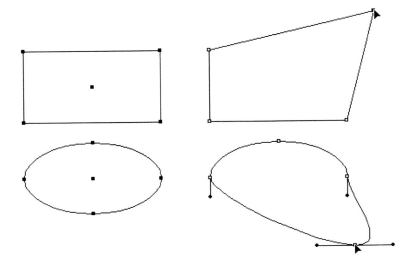

In a high-end program, you ungroup a geometric object in order edit its path.

On the left are a (grouped) rectangle and oval created in Adobe Illustrator. The shapes on the right have been ungrouped and reshaped.

In more conventional drawing programs, you cannot reshape most geometric objects. The only exception is the rectangle with rounded corners, which you may adjust either by choosing a "Round Corners" command or using a reshape tool. Some programs even provide a special handle for reshaping rectangles as you drag.

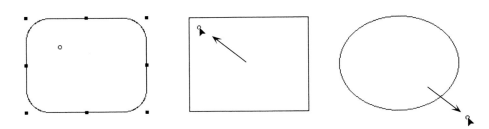

In a program like Canvas, we drag the reshape handle up and to the left to reduce the size of rounded corners, or drag the handle down and to the right to increase the radius of all corners.

True reshaping features, however, are generally applicable only to free-form paths created with the freehand, polygon, or Bézier curve tool. We will first examine how to alter the points in such paths.

Moving points

After you have displayed the points in a free-form path using the arrow or reshape tool, you may manipulate them. To move a single point in a path, simply select the point and drag it to a new location. The segment connecting this point and its neighbors will stretch or shrink accordingly.

Many programs allow you to move more than one point at a time. First select the additional points by pressing the shift key and clicking on the points. Or drag at an empty portion of your screen to create a rectangular marquee around the points you want to select. Then drag the selected points to move them.

When you move a point, its segments stretch or shrink like taut rubber bands.

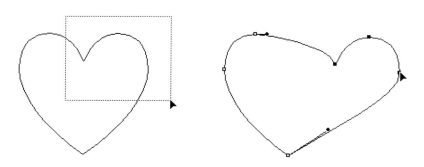

One way to select multiple point is to marquee them, as shown on the left. You may then move the selected points by dragging any one of them.

Move a point when you want to change the location of a corner or the position of a curve. Programs that offer a Bézier curve tool also allow you to alter the curvature of a segment by adjusting the location of the Bézier control handles relative to their points.

Adjusting curved segments

To display Bézier control handles for a point, you typically select the point in your program's reshape mode. To adjust the curvature of a segment, drag the tip of the Bézier control handle in much the same way you would drag a point. Keep the control handle close to its point to create slight curves; drag the control handle farther away for more extreme curves.

To adjust the curvature of a segment, drag the tip of a Bézier control handle as you would drag a point.

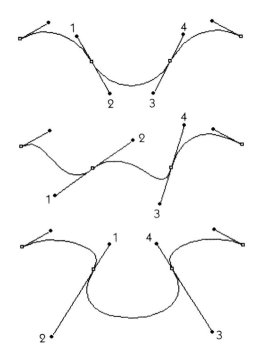

Here we have created three versions of the same path. In each case, we have adjusted the location of the numbered Bézier control handles.

Some programs even allow you to drag on the segment itself to alter its curvature. The Bézier control handles adjust automatically.

One of the most common problems that most users have when learning drawing software is trying to determine the placement of

Developing a Successful Drawing Technique

Bézier control handles. Several rules have been developed over the years, but the best are the *all-or-nothing rule* and the *30% rule*. The all-or-nothing rule states that every segment in your path should be associated with either two Bézier control handles or none at all. In other words, no segment should rely on only one control handle to determine its curvature. In the 30% rule, the distance from any Bézier control handle to its point should be approximately 30% the length of the segment.

A curved segment should be bounded by a Bézier control handle on both sides.

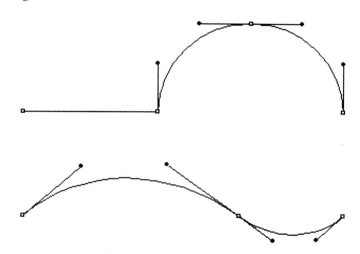

The top path demonstrates the all-or-nothing rule. The straight segment is associated with no control handle, while both curved segments have two handles apiece. The bottom path demonstrates the 30% rule. The two control handles belonging to the left segment each take up about 30% of the length of the segment. The right segment is shorter, so its handles are shorter as well.

Moving points and adjusting control handles are fundamental ways to change the shape of a path. But sometimes, no matter how long you spend adjusting the placement of its points or the curvature of its segments, a path fails to meet the requirements of your drawing. In this case, you may want to expand the path by adding points or simplify the path by deleting points.

Adding and deleting points

All drawing programs let you add and delete points in a path. Some applications allow you to add a point to the end of an open line. Others allow you only to insert a point into an existing segment. But either way, you can extend a path to a more functional length as described in the following figure captions.

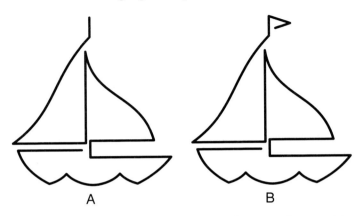

A   B

Suppose we want to add a tiny flag to boat A, thus making it look like boat B. The simplest way to do this would be to append two corner points to the end of the path.

If you can't add a point to the end of a line, insert a point near the end and move the points into position.

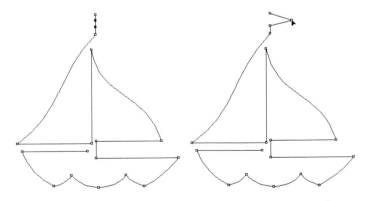

However, if you use a program, such as MacDraw, that doesn't allow you to extend a path, you may insert points in the last segment of the path and then move the points into position as shown above.

The specific method for adding a point depends on your software. In Adobe Illustrator, you insert a point into a segment by pressing the option key while clicking on the segment with the scissors tool. In Aldus FreeHand, you simply click on the segment with the Bézier curve tool. In most conventional drawing programs, you press a modifier key, such as option, and click on a segment while in the reshape mode. In Canvas, you choose a special "Add Pnts" command.

The technique for deleting a point from a path is similar to that for adding a point; it also depends on your software. In many applications, you select the point and press the delete key. In others, you press a modifier key and click. In Canvas, you choose a special "Delete Pnts" command.

Deleting a point generally does not break the path. Instead, a new segment connects the two points neighboring the deleted point.

Suppose you want to delete the black point in the first path above. When you delete a point in most programs, a new segment automatically connects its neighbors, as demonstrated by the middle image. But in Adobe Illustrator, deleting a point also deletes any associated segment, leaving a break in the path, as shown on the right. To repair the break, drag at both points with the Bézier curve tool.

In most drawing programs, you can add points, delete points, join points, and split a point in two.

Adding and deleting points aren't the only ways to reshape a path. Your program probably also provides commands for deleting segments and joining two paths into one, as well as other reshaping techniques. But for now, you will find that the path manipulation features covered in this chapter are more than enough to get you started. Knowing how to add or delete a point is no great feat; you'll have these features figured out after experimenting with them only a couple of times. The real trick is to know how many points you need in a curve, and where to place them. By working only with the few reshaping tools mentioned so far, you can better concentrate on developing your drawing technique.

The ability to reshape a line after it is created is unique to the computer graphics environment. The fact that no scribble is permanent, regardless of how long ago it was created, stands in direct opposition to many traditional media. By comparison, an ink line or brush stroke may just as well be etched in stone.

But reshaping is merely one aspect of your manipulative powers in a drawing program. Images may be moved, enlarged, reduced, rotated, and transformed in many other ways, depending on the sophistication of your software. Your software's potential for special effects will absolutely boggle your mind.

In a drawing program, both free-form and geometric elements may be moved, copied, stretched, and rotated.

Transforming objects

Regardless of what tool you used to create it, any graphic element in a drawing application can be moved, copied, or otherwise manipulated. The most popular transformation tools allow you to scale, flip, rotate, or skew an image any number of times and to any extent imaginable.

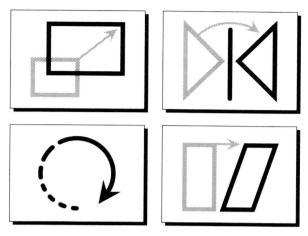

The transformation tools are the primary means of manipulating entire paths in a drawing program.

The following pages describe how to use these tools, including how to select, move, clone, copy, and apply several popular commands to a path or group of paths.

Selecting and grouping

Most transformations are applicable only to entire paths, rather than to their points or segments. For example, although you can move a handful of selected points, you probably cannot enlarge or rotate them. Therefore, before you can transform a free-form or geometric path, you must select the entire object.

In most programs, you select an entire path simply by clicking on it with the arrow tool. Only in Adobe Illustrator does it work differently. In this program, you press the option key and click anywhere on the path to select the whole path.

To select multiple paths, click on the first path, then press the shift key and click on all additional paths. Or use the arrow tool to drag at an empty portion of your screen and create a rectangular

To select multiple paths, click on the first path, then press the shift key while clicking on additional paths.

marquee around the paths you want to select. (In Adobe Illustrator, press the option key while shift-selecting or marqueeing to select multiple whole paths.)

Suppose you have created an image made up of several paths, and you're afraid of upsetting the fragile relationship between these paths during a transformation. To safeguard the basic appearance of the image, you can group it into a single object using your program's "Group" command.

Choose the "Group" command to combine objects that you intend to transform as a single image.

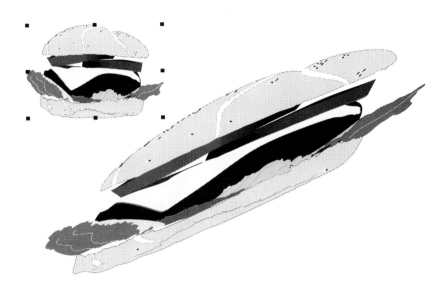

This hamburger image contains over one hundred paths. To retain the relationships between these paths, we group them into a single object, as indicated by the transformation handles surrounding the first image. We can then stretch, skew, and rotate the image without fear of disrupting its basic hamburger appearance.

Once your object or objects are grouped and selected, you can apply one or more of the transformations discussed in the following pages.

Deleting, moving, and layering

The primary purposes for selecting any graphic element are to move the element to a new location and to delete it from the page. Because both of these transformations are so common, they are extremely simple to apply.

To delete an object from your drawing, simply select it and press the delete key. The element will disappear from your page. Generally, you should delete an object only if you are completely dissatisfied with it and you are positive you'll never need it again. (You may restore an object immediately after deleting it by choosing the "Undo" command before beginning another operation.) If you think you might need a graphic element later, but you want to get it out of the way for now, a better solution is to choose the "Cut" command and send the object to your program's clipboard for temporary storage. Both the "Cut" command and the clipboard are discussed in more detail later in this section.

To move an object, click and drag it with your arrow tool cursor. When you have repositioned the object to a new location, release the mouse button.

Rather than moving an object up or down or left or right, you may sometimes want to move it in front of or behind another object. This third-dimensional relationship between objects is called *layering*. For example, suppose you have drawn a series of paths and grouped them into two objects: a piece of chalk and a slate. For the chalk to appear as if it were writing on the slate, the chalk object should be layered in front of the slate object. But, if instead, the slate object is the foremost of the two, you must either select the slate object and choose a "Send to back" command or select the chalk object and choose "Bring to front."

You may move an object in front of or behind another object by choosing a layering command.

Slate is layered in front of chalk in the drawing on the left. To correct this layering problem, we select the paths that make up the piece of chalk and choose the "Bring to front" command.

The "Cut" and "Copy" commands send the selected image to the clipboard for temporary storage.

When you move an object, whether to a new position on the page or to a different layer, you effectively delete it from its previous location. However, if you prefer, you may retain an element at its original location and at the same time move it by applying one of several duplication techniques.

Duplication techniques

The "Cut," "Copy," and "Paste" commands are available in any Macintosh application. The "Cut" and "Copy" commands store a selected image so it may be used later in the drawing process. The "Paste" command retrieves the stored image as a selected object that may then be moved to any location in your drawing.

Each command works with Apple's built-in *clipboard*, which is capable of storing a single image at a time. The "Cut" command removes the selected objects from your graphic and places them in the clipboard, simultaneously erasing the clipboard's previous image. The "Copy" command also replaces the clipboard's previous image, but does not delete the selected objects from your graphic. The "Paste" command retrieves a copy of the clipboard image and imports the objects into your drawing.

All three commands are useful for duplicating objects during the creation of a drawing. You may also use these commands to transfer objects into other applications. However, if you want to create a single copy of an object that you intend to use immediately, most applications offer a quicker means of duplication known as *cloning*.

To clone an object is to create a quick copy of it without displacing the current contents of the clipboard. Clones are very simple to create in almost every drawing application: Merely select an object, press the option key, and drag the selected object to a new location. By pressing the option key, one copy of the object remains at its original location while the other selected copy is created at the point where you release your mouse button.

Pressing the option key allows you to create a clone for every time you drag and release the mouse button.

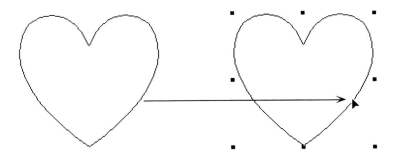

To clone an object, press the option key and drag the selected object to a new location.

Cloning is a useful and efficient technique for creating multiple copies of objects. Each clone may then be transformed separately, depending on your particular graphic requirements. The following text describes the kinds of transformations you may apply to an object.

Scaling an object

To *scale* an object is to enlarge or reduce it to another size. In most drawing applications, you scale an object by dragging at one of its eight transformation handles. Dragging a handle away from the object enlarges its size; dragging a handle toward an object reduces it. You stretch an object vertically or horizontally by dragging at one of the four side handles. In this way, you may produce tall, skinny objects, or short, fat ones. To scale an object proportionally, press the shift key and drag at a corner handle.

Enlarge or reduce an object by dragging at one of its transformation handles.

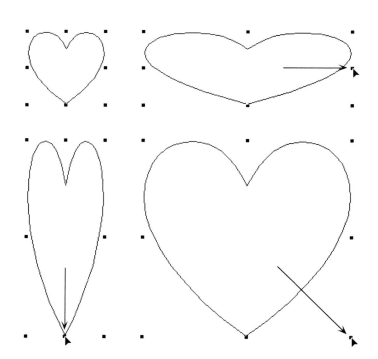

In most programs, you scale an object by dragging at one of its transformation handles.

Not all drawing applications allow you to scale an object by dragging at one of its handles. In a program like Adobe Illustrator, for example, you must use a special scale tool. You first click near the center of the selected object with the tool to establish a scale origin. You then position your cursor near one of the corners and drag to scale the object. (Illustrator also provides tools for flipping, rotating, and skewing a selected object; such tools function according to this same click-and-drag technique.)

Flipping an object

In many drawing programs, reducing an element too far, either by using a scale tool or by dragging a transformation handle, flips the object to create a mirror image.

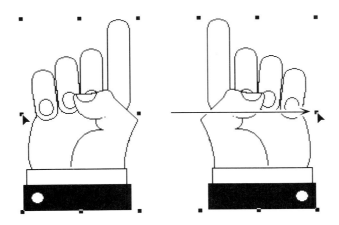

To flip the grouped image shown above in a program like MacDraw, we drag the left transformation handle all the way across to the right side of the image.

In some programs, reducing an image too far in one direction will flip it to create a mirror image.

Other applications provide "Flip horizontal" and "Flip vertical" commands. Each command creates a mirror image of the selected object. To create an upside-down image, choose both the "Flip horizontal" and "Flip vertical" commands.

Rotating an object

The "Rotate" command works differently in different applications. In some programs, choosing the command displays a dialog box. You enter a number of degrees between 0 and 360, click the OK button, and the software rotates the selected object according to your specification. (A degree is $\frac{1}{360}$ circle, measured in a counterclockwise direction.)

In other programs, choosing the "Rotate" command displays a special rotation cursor. You then drag one of the corner transformation handles in a clockwise or counterclockwise direction to rotate the selected object in single-degree increments. You may constrain the angle your rotation to a multiple of 45° (one-eighth turn) by pressing the shift key while dragging a handle.

You can generally rotate objects in one- degree increments, a degree being $\frac{1}{360}$ circle.

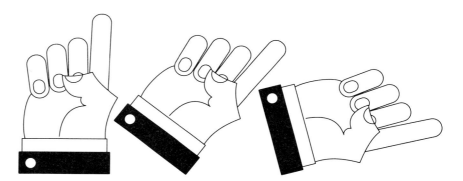

Most drawing programs allow you to rotate a selected image to any angle you desire.

Still other programs, like Adobe Illustrator and Aldus FreeHand, provide a rotation tool. Click to establish a rotation origin, then drag around this origin to rotate the selected object.

Skewing an object

The "Slant" or "Skew" command is not available in all drawing programs. But when available, it generally works very much like the "Rotate" command. You first choose "Slant" or "Skew" to display a special skew cursor. Then drag one of the side transformation handles horizontally or vertically to slant the selected object in single-degree increments.

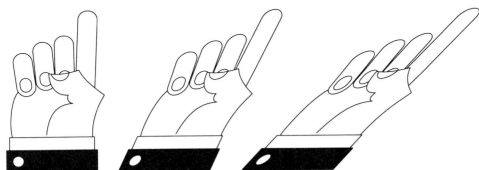

The "Skew" command differs from "Rotate" in that it tips an object backward or forward rather than spinning it around in a circle.

The skew command is useful for creating slanted text and perspective effects.

Some programs, like Adobe Illustrator and Aldus FreeHand, provide a skew tool. Click to establish a skew origin, then drag with respect to this origin to slant the selected object. Press the shift key to constrain the skew horizontally or vertically.

The "Skew" command is especially useful for creating slanted text. You may also combine skewing with scaling to produce a perspective effect.

Multiple transformation techniques can be combined to create spectacular special effects.

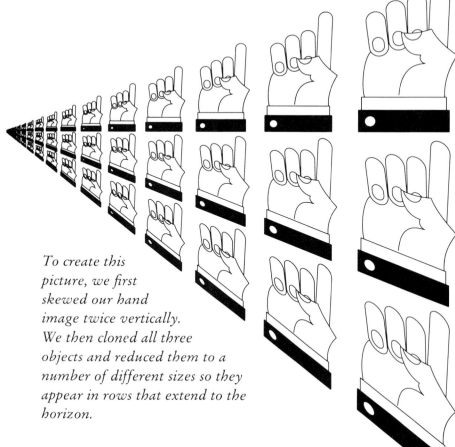

To create this picture, we first skewed our hand image twice vertically. We then cloned all three objects and reduced them to a number of different sizes so they appear in rows that extend to the horizon.

Don't be afraid to apply a combination of transformation techniques to the same image in order to achieve perspective. In addition to skewing and scaling, many programs allow you to clone an object while otherwise transforming it by pressing the option key as you drag. You may then choose a "Duplicate" command to repeat both the clone and transformation operation any number of times. If this sounds like too much to take in at once, you will want to experiment with the sample projects included in Chapters 5 through 7. Each chapter contains step-by-step transformation examples with increasing levels of difficulty.

Developing a Successful Drawing Technique

To recap, you select objects with the arrow tool. If you want to apply a series of transformations to an image made up of multiple paths, select all paths and group them before applying any other command.

You may move a selected object by dragging it. You may also duplicate one or more paths using the "Cut," "Copy," and "Paste" commands or by pressing the option key and dragging to create a clone.

Use your software's transformation commands to create special effects. For example, you may use scaling to create an enlarged or miniaturized version of an object. You can also make objects fatter or thinner by scaling. If you want to create a mirror image of an object to create a shadow or reflection, choose the "Flip horizontal" or "Flip vertical" command. Rotate an object when you want to tilt it at some angle. This is especially useful if you want to turn an image upside down or otherwise experiment with its positioning. And finally, you can skew an object to make it slant horizontally or vertically, or to lend depth to your drawing through perspective.

This completes our discussion of creating and manipulating graphic elements. The last section of this chapter discusses how to use type in a drawing program, and how to fill and stroke your type and graphics.

The type tool and font commands

Your program's type tool is actually just another drawing tool, like the freehand or Bézier curve tool. While most programs do not allow you to reshape text, you can transform it as discussed in the previous section, and you can fill and stroke it, as we will discuss in the next section.

In a drawing program, text is just another graphic element that can be moved, duplicated, and transformed.

The type tool allows you to enter text from the keyboard in your graphic.

In the next few pages, we will discuss how to add type to your graphic. We will also examine specific features that are applicable only to text—typeface (also called font), size, style, and kerning. Finally, we will look at creating text on a curve.

Entering type from the keyboard

To create a block of text, click with the type tool at the point in your graphic where you want your text to begin. In most programs, a blinking text entry cursor will appear where you have clicked, indicating that the application is ready for you to begin typing. In a few high-end applications, such as Aldus FreeHand and Adobe Illustrator, a dialog box will appear, providing a special text-entry area.

As you enter text from your keyboard, the characters will appear on your screen. The text entry cursor moves as you type, always indicating the location of the next character. If you make a mistake, you may move your text entry cursor within a text block by pressing one of the cursor arrow keys ($\uparrow$, $\leftarrow$, $\downarrow$, $\rightarrow$). This useful feature allows you to move the text entry cursor back to the location of a mistake and fix it without altering any correct text.

You may move your cursor from one character to another in a text block using the arrow keys.

Now iz the time for

Now i the time for

Now is the time for

If you notice a typographic error while entering text, you may use your arrow keys to navigate back to where the error occurred, correct it, and navigate forward again.

Also, most drawing applications do not allow you to indicate column widths for text. Instead, you must press the return key to begin a new line of type.

To complete a text block, select a different tool, such as the arrow tool, or click the OK button in the text entry dialog box. Any additional letters entered from the keyboard will no longer appear on your screen.

When entering text from the keyboard, you generally press the return or enter key to begin a new line of type.

Editing and correcting text

After you finish creating a block of text in a drawing program, you can always edit it later. This is useful if you discover a typographical error you overlooked when entering the text, or you want to change the font or type size, as we will discuss later in this section.

Text must be *highlighted* to be edited. In most drawing programs, you highlight text with the type tool by dragging directly over the words you want to change. In programs that offer a text entry dialog box, you select your text block with the arrow tool and choose a text editing command. In Adobe Illustrator, choose the "Type" command. In Aldus FreeHand, choose "Element info" or double-click the text block. Once inside the dialog box, drag over the text you want to edit with your text entry cursor. Regardless of the program you use, the highlighted text will appear as white type against a black background.

Now is the time for

In most programs, you select text by dragging over it with the type tool. Here we have dragged from just after the "o" in "Now" up to and including the "m" in "time."

To edit a word, you must first highlight it by dragging over it with your cursor.

Some applications offer shortcuts for highlighting text. For example, double-clicking often highlights an entire word. Also, once the text entry point has been set, pressing the shift key and clicking at another location will sometimes highlight all text between the original entry point and the new entry point.

If you type any keys on your keyboard, you will replace the highlighted text. Therefore, if you highlight a single word, you can replace it with a new word simply by typing. Or you may delete one or more words by pressing the delete key.

Note for

After highlighting the text shown in the previous figure, we pressed the T key, replacing the highlighted text with a new letter.

By replacing highlighted text with new text, you can correct and edit blocks of type. But you can also use highlighting to change text attributes, such as typeface, size, and style.

Developing a Successful Drawing Technique

Formatting text

At any time in the drawing process, you may change the formatting of one or more letters of text by highlighting them and applying font commands. In a typical drawing program, formatting includes typeface, style, size, leading, and alignment. Your choices in each of these formatting categories may affect the entire block of text or only the highlighted portions.

Typeface is the most important formatting attribute, since it sets the mood for the text. Typically, fonts are chosen as commands from a menu or from a list within a dialog box. The font that you choose will alter the appearance of each character in a block of text.

Avant Garde Book

Bookman Demibold

Courier

Helvetica Oblique

Palatino Roman

Narrow Helvetica Bold

New Century Schoolbook

αℜ⊗Σ∫Ω (Symbol)

Times Bold

Zapf Chancery Medium Italic

✏✗✠❣➪✈ (Zapf Dingbats)

The font that you choose will alter the appearance of each character in a block of text.

More and more typefaces are becoming available to desktop publishers. The fonts shown above are some of those most commonly available to PostScript printers.

The variety and number of typefaces available in your drawing application is determined directly by the contents of your System file. Fonts can be added to or deleted from your System file using Apple's Font/DA Mover utility. For complete information on configuring your System, consult your Macintosh owner's manual.

You may also choose from a variety of type styles—as determined by your application—to slightly alter the appearance of the current typeface. "Plain" is the normal type style, and should be chosen if you want the font to appear "as is," unaltered in any way. "Bold" and "Italic" are common styles of a font, often included as part of the typeface family. For example, Times Roman is the plain style of the font Times. Times Bold and Times Italic are distinct typefaces but are part of the same type family. It is also possible to combine "Bold" and "Italic," in this case creating Times Bold Italic. If no bold or italic style is specifically designed for a typeface—for example, the Zapf Dingbats family includes only plain Dingbats—most drawing applications will print the font normally, even if you choose "Bold," "Italic," or both.

Plain
Bold
Italic
Bold Italic
<u>Underline</u>
Outline
Bold Outline
Shadow
Bold Shadow

Above are combinations of type styles available in many drawing applications. Any style can be applied to any font; every style, except for "Plain," can be combined with any other style.

Type styles can be used to enhance the appearance of a typeface.

Some applications include other type styles such as "Underline," "Outline," and "Shadow," none of which rely on type family definitions but are instead applied to any typeface by the drawing program itself.

Type size determines the height of the letters in a text block. Size is measured in points, tiny units equal to $\frac{1}{72}$ of an inch. Size availability typically ranges from 4-point to 500-point, or even higher. Although various type sizes may not appear particularly legibly on your screen, the type will always look smooth and readable when printed.

108-point

81-point

54-point

36-point

27-point

18-point

Shown here is a sample of the type sizes available in a drawing application. All sizes are shown in the font Helvetica.

12-point

9-point

6-point

4-point

The fourth category of text formatting in drawing applications is *leading* (pronounced lĕd·ing), which is the amount of vertical space between one line of type and the next line in the same text block. Many programs allow for leading values accurate to ⅒ point.

The leading of this text is 12-point (solid).

The leading of this text block is 13-point.

The leading of this text is 14.4-point (auto).

The leading of this text block is 16-point.

The leading of this text block is 18-point.

The leading of this text block is 24-point.

Shown above are blocks of 12-point type with different leadings. The first block has solid leading, since the type size and leading values are equal. Generally, type looks best when the leading is about 20% larger than the type size, sometimes called "auto" leading.

Leading is the amount of vertical spacing between lines of text.

Advanced drawing programs like Aldus FreeHand allow you to control the *kerning*—the amount of horizontal space between pairs of letters. Being able to adjust kerning is especially useful in the creation of large text and logos, in which a font's normal letter spacing creates a noticeable gap between a capital character with an overhang, such as *T,* and a small lowercase character, like *o.*

The last formatting category is *alignment.* Alignment determines the relative positioning of each line of type within a block of text. Type is aligned with reference to the point where you originally clicked with the type tool. Generally, your click location determines the leftmost point of text that is aligned left or is justified, the rightmost point of type that is aligned right, and the center point of type that is aligned middle, or centered.

Tomorrow
Yesterday

Tomorrow
Yesterday

In the first two words, we rely on standard letter spacing. Because our text is so large, you can see inconsistent gaps between the first two letters in both words. In the bottom examples, we have tightened the kerning between each of the first two pairs of letters. Other pairs have been adjusted as well to streamline the overall appearance of the text.

This text is ragged right, also called flush left.

This text is ragged left, also called flush right.

This text is aligned middle, also called centered.

Type in a typical drawing application may be flush left, flush right, centered, or justified.

This text is fully justified, flush on both the left and right sides.

Text is generally aligned in relation to the point at which you clicked with the type tool.

Font, style, size, leading, kerning, and alignment work together to determine the basic appearance of your text block. Each formatting category affects only the text that is currently highlighted. The one exception is alignment, which typically affects an entire text block.

Text on a path

Perhaps the most exciting way to use text in a drawing program is to make it follow the course of a free-form path.

Text adheres to a path based on its current alignment; justified text stretches to fill the length of the path.

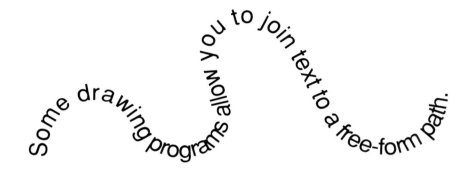

This one speaks for itself.

Only a few applications, like Aldus FreeHand, provide this capability. If yours does not, you may achieve similar—albeit much more laborious—effects by carefully rotating and positioning individual characters.

To fit text to a path, select both the text block and the path and choose "Join" or an equivalent command. The text will adhere to the path based on the way it is aligned, that is, whether the text is flush left, centered, or so on.

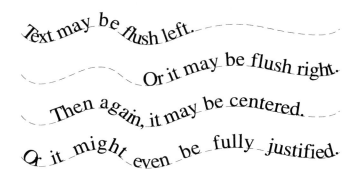

Alignment determines how the text positions on the path.

If your path involves many twists and turns, you will have to kern some letters to make your text legible. Letters curve apart from each other as they pass over convex curves, while they tend to overlap when passing through concave curves. If you tighten the kerning in the convex areas and loosen the kerning in the concave areas, your letter spacing will appear more consistent.

Kern between characters to avoid tight type in concave curves and loose type across convex curves.

Some drawing programs allow you to join text to a free-form path.

In the figure on the facing page, some letters overlap while others appear too loose. By kerning these letters, we have created more consistent free-form type, as shown above. Below that, we have separated the text from the path to demonstrate how the kerning was applied.

Beware of relying too completely on your software's automated features. Just because you can fit text to a path doesn't mean it will look good. In fact, complicated paths almost always produce illegible or ugly text. However time-consuming kerning may be, you are always better off kerning your text to even out the letter spacing, to give it a "fluid" touch.

———————————◆◆◆———————————

Generally, we recommend that you enter only small amounts of display text in a drawing application. Large amounts of body copy text should be input in a word processor, in which you can format text more quickly and check your spelling.

Remember that the only advantage to text typed directly in a drawing program over text created in a word processor is that the former may be manipulated graphically. You can create many attractive effects by transforming type, joining type to a curve, and applying stroke and fill combinations as discussed in the following section. For additional ideas, refer to the *Type effects* section of Chapter 4.

Stroke determines the appearance of a shape's outline, fill determines the appearance of a shape's interior.

Applying strokes and fills

Drawing programs provide two ways to apply colors to your lines, shapes, and text blocks. *Stroke* determines the thickness and color of the outline of a path or character of type. *Fill* determines the color of the interior of a graphic element or type.

Your software's stroke and fill features, whether provided as tools or commands, allow you to add color to your drawings.

The remaining pages discuss how to apply strokes and fills to any object created in a drawing program.

The weight of a line or outline

Applying a stroke to a path is much like adding ink to a pencil sketch. A stroke adds dimension and polish to your drawing. And like lines created with professional drawing pens, computer-generated strokes come in different colors and thicknesses. In a drawing program, these thickness are called *line weights*.

Select a line weight to determine the thickness of a stroke.

| 0.3-point (hairline) |
| 0.5-point |
| 1-point |
| 2-point |
| 4-point |
| 6-point (half pica) |
| 8-point |
| 12-point (one pica) |
| 24-point (two picas) |

Shown above are a handful of common line weights.

Some programs even allow you to apply a line weight to a block of text in order to control the thickness of outlined letters.

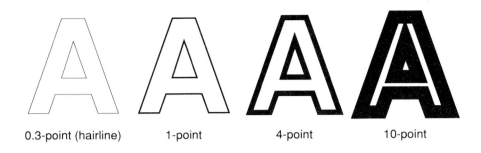

0.3-point (hairline)   1-point   4-point   10-point

In programs that allow you to apply a stroke to a block of text, you may determine the weight of outline type.

Line weight is commonly measured in points. Most drawing applications allow you to create any line weight from 0.02-point—the thinnest line printable by the highest resolution typesetter—to over an inch thick.

Line weights can be used to trace the outlines of both geometric and free-form paths. More sophisticated applications even allow you to stroke individual letters in a text block, as shown above. Depending on your program, you may be able to specify additional stroking variations, such as dotted lines and arrowheads, as we will describe in the following text.

Corners, caps, and dashes

Many drawing programs provide options for determining the appearance of the stroke of a path. For example, you may determine how the stroke appears at sharp corners in a shape. Normally, when two segments meet to form a sharp corner, the stroke extends to a sharp point as well. However, if your path includes very sharp corners—with angles smaller than 10°—the stroke has to extend well beyond the corner point, sometimes encroaching on other portions of your drawing. This phenomenon is especially noticeable when two oppositely curving segments meet in a corner point.

Developing a Successful Drawing Technique

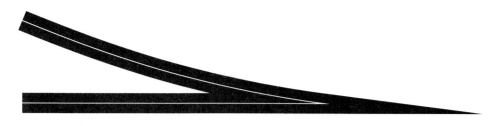

In this figure, the path is displayed as white and the stroke is displayed as black. Notice that the path runs through the exact middle of the stroke. A curved segment bends toward a straight segment, finally meeting it at an angle of less than 2°. As a result, the stroke is forced to extend a distance of several times its weight beyond the corner of the path.

To control the appearance of a corner formed by two curved segments, you may apply one of three *joining* options to their strokes. A *miter join* forces the stroke to form a sharp corner, as shown above. The alternates are the *round join*, which smooths off corners to give your paths a soft appearance, and the *bevel join*, which severs the stroke abruptly at the corner point.

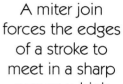

A miter join forces the edges of a stroke to meet in a sharp corner, which sometimes encroaches on other images.

Line joins determine the appearance of a stroke at a corner point in a path. The stroke may be mitered to taper to a point, or rounded, or beveled. All three joins are shown above.

Similarly, you can control how a line ends using one of four *cap* options. The default *butt cap* ends where the path ends, perpendicular to the final segment. The *round cap*, used almost exclusively with the round join, appends a semicircle to the final point of a path. The *square cap* is perpendicular, like the butt cap, but extends half the line weight past the end of the path. And the *arrow cap* creates an arrow-head at one or both ends of a line. In some programs, you may edit the exact shape and size of an arrow cap.

Line caps
determine how
a stroke
behaves at
the first and
last points
in a path.

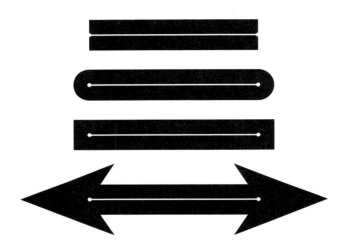

The four line caps include the butt cap, the round cap, the square cap, and the arrow cap. The white lines demonstrate the orientation of the paths in relation to the strokes.

Finally, you may create regular interruptions in the stroke of a path by applying a *dash pattern*. In most programs, you simply choose a dash pattern from a menu of dotted lines. In Adobe Illustrator and Aldus FreeHand, however, you may enter values to specify the length of each dash and each gap in the pattern.

Each of the line caps, with the exception of the arrow cap, also affect the beginning and ending of each dash.

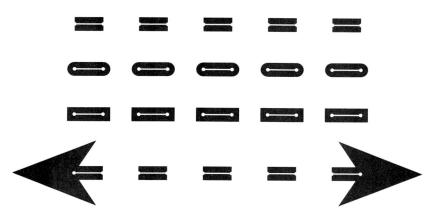

The butt cap, round cap, and square cap affect the beginning and ending of each dash in a dash pattern stroke. The arrow cap, however, affects only the ends of the path.

To create perfectly round dashes, your dash pattern must have a dash zero points long and a gap about twice the size of the line weight. Here we have a line weight of 12 point and a dash pattern of 0 on and 24 off.

A dash pattern is used most commonly to indicate a cut-out line, as in the case of coupons or paper dolls. But it may also be used to stroke a ghostly image or one that it transparent in nature.

You may apply a stroke to any line or outline of a shape. You may also fill the interior of a shape. Typically, you may not assign a fill to an open path, since it has no interior. Fills are applicable only if the path forms a continuous, unbroken outline.

Line caps also control the way in which a dash begins and ends, so that you can create a path composed of round dots.

Filling shapes with tints

You may fill a shape with either solid color or a *tint*. A tint is a cluster of dots that emulates a shade of gray or a lightened shade of a color. The color of each dot determines the color of the tint. A tint of black dots appears gray, red dots appear pink, and so on.

Gray values and colors are printed as a pattern of tiny round dots, arranged into a grid of halftone cells.

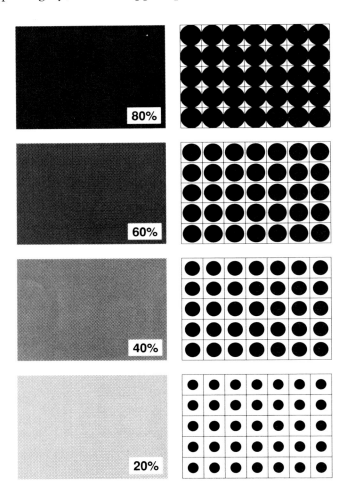

On the left are four tints. Although each one looks like a shade of gray, it is actually a collection of tiny black dots. On the right, these dots are blown up to 20 times their normal size. The squares represent the boundaries of the halftone cells.

Developing a Successful Drawing Technique

The dots are arranged into a grid of *halftone cells*, much like a checkerboard. The dots grow and shrink inside their halftone cells to emulate different shades of color. Large dots create dark tints and small dots make light tints.

Tints are specified in terms of percentages. If an area is filled with a 50% black tint, each dot fills half the area of its halftone cell.

Filling shapes with solid colors and tints is a quick and easy task in any drawing program. However, few images in real life appear to be filled with a single, flat color. To produce more exciting, realistic textural fills, you might want to examine your program's collection of bitmapped and object-oriented patterns.

Creating textural patterns

Patterns are similar to tints, but slightly more complicated. Rather than containing dot sequences, patterns tend to repeat a simple object or design. Drawing programs such as MacDraw and Aldus FreeHand supply you with a library of bitmapped patterns. Library sizes vary dramatically from program to program. See the following page for samples patterns taken from a variety of drawing applications.

Despite the proliferation of patterns at your disposal, you may want to modify an existing bitmapped pattern or create one of your own. Generally, this involves double-clicking a pattern icon or choosing an "Edit pattern" command. A dialog box will appear, allowing you to adjust the dots that make up a pattern.

Patterns that mimic wood grain or fish scales can add realistic texture to an image.

Bitmapped patterns are easy to create and edit, but they appear jagged when printed.

Bitmapped patterns range from the sedate to the ostenta-tious. Some patterns are useful primarily for shading, like those containing straight and diagonal lines shown in the top portion of the figure. Others represent real-life patterns, like bricks, fish scales, basket weave, tiles, shingles, and so on.

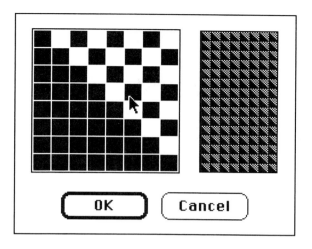

This is an example of a dialog box that permits you to edit patterns. The left view of the pattern, which is magnified, shows the square grid of dots that will be repeated over and over to create the pattern. The right view demonstrates the actual size of the pattern, repeated many times. You may alter the pattern by clicking on and off the dots on the left while observing the results of your editing on the right.

Advanced programs also allow you to create object-oriented patterns that print more smoothly than the ones we have seen so far. Typically, you create such a pattern by drawing a single rectangular *tile*. The program then repeats this tile throughout the interior of a shape, like the tiles on a kitchen floor.

Object-oriented patterns require that you arrange images into rectangular tiles, which appear continuous when placed side by side.

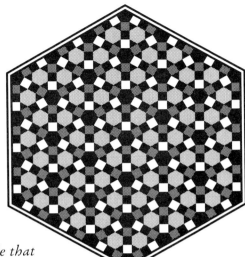

*On the left, we have
created a rectangular tile that
will appear continuous when placed
next to itself top to bottom or side to side.
The tile is then reduced and repeated throughout the
interior of the shape on the right to produce an elegant
geometric pattern.*

The purpose
of a pattern is to
enhance your
drawing, not to
overwhelm it.

Try altering a few patterns before you create one from scratch. But whether altering or creating a pattern, consider not only the pattern's immediate quality—how it will impress your viewer—but also its chance of integrating into your graphic. Keep in mind that the purpose of patterns is to enhance your drawings, not to overwhelm them.

Gradations and masking

A few high-end drawing programs provide additional fill features to facilitate the creation of realistic images. For example, Aldus Free-Hand offers automated *gradation* commands for creating fills that fade from one color to another. Gradations are extremely useful for representing the volume of a shape, which we discussed in Chapter 2.

Gradations can fade from right to left or from left to right. To fill our fish shapes, we simply specified a tint for the beginning color and another for the ending color, and let the software do the work.

Gradations are fills that fade seamlessly from one color to another.

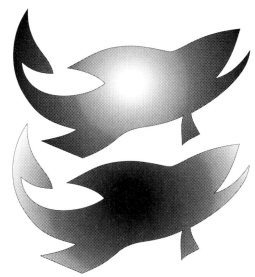

Radial gradations begin at the center of the shape and progress outward in concentric circles. The gradation in the first fish begins with white and ends in black. The beginning and ending colors are switched to create the second fish.

Unfortunately, even automated gradations can be limiting. You can't determine the exact point at which a gradation begins or ends, and you may use only two colors. You can create a fill that fades from light blue to dark blue, but not from light blue to dark blue to green to brown. Also, you have no control over the shape of the individual bands of color. They are arranged either as straight lines or as concentric circles.

To compensate for the limits of automated gradations, *masking* has become such a popular drawing software feature. Using masking, you can fill one object, called a *mask*, with several others. The mask acts as a cookie cutter, clipping away those portions of other line and shapes that don't fit inside it. You may create truly custom fills for any object, filling paths with text or text with paths.

A mask acts as a cookie cutter, clipping away those portions of other paths that don't fit inside it.

In this example, the heart acts as a mask. We then fill the heart shape with a custom gradation and a block of text. As you can see, simple objects such as this valentine make great masks because they don't compete with their contents.

William Blake

Some applications even allow you to turn a block of text into a mask. An infinite variety of type effects are possible with this feature.

In a sophisticated program, paths can mask type and letters can mask images.

While the specific method for creating a mask varies from software to software, all features share certain similarities. You first stroke and fill the objects that you want to mask using solid colors and tints. You then select the path or type which will serve as the mask and apply your program's "Mask" command, or the equivalent. Finally, combine the mask with its prospective contents. The result will be a professional-quality image rivaling just about anything you could create using traditional inking and airbrushing techniques.

If your software does not provide a masking feature, see the *Custom interiors* section of Chapter 4 for an alternate technique.

Stroke and fill effects can dress up your images, changing meaningless paths and text into realistic images that will entertain and excite viewers.

Stroke defines the outline of an image. Thick line weights make an object stand out from those around it. Thin line weights allow one path to blend naturally with another. Caps and joins can be used to soften an image or exaggerate its harsh edges.

When filling a shape, consider your options carefully, balancing the excitement of a lively pattern against the safety of a conservative solid color or tint. Usually, you can select the appropriate pattern from those provided in your drawing program. But occasionally, you will have to modify an existing pattern or create a new one.

After you've accumulated sufficient experience with stroke and fill effects, you will want to experiment with masking. By filling one object with many others, you can heighten the realism of your artwork. As in real life, your most successful pictures will be those that integrate hundreds of elements into a single cohesive whole.

CHAPTER 4

Tips and Drawing Secrets

In the previous chapter we discussed how to operate the basic tools and commands available in most drawing applications. Although this knowledge is fundamental to creating a successful computer illustration, few of us think in terms of tools or commands. Instead, we think about results, and rightly so. The question is not, *What kind of drawing will I create if I do this and this and this?*, but rather, *What must I do to satisfactorily complete this drawing?*

Each of the
following
examples
demonstrates
how to use tools
and commands
to achieve
a goal.

This chapter also deals with results. Rather than outlining the specific uses of individual tools and commands, each of the following examples demonstrates how to combine multiple tools and commands to achieve a particular goal. Such a goal might be the solution to a problem that you have encountered often. Or it might be simply a special effect that you have not considered previously. All examples are designed to span any graphic type, and most work with even the most rudimentary drawing application.

Each goal is introduced in detail, and we explain why it is important and how it fits into the larger concept of a finished illustration. This introduction is followed by one or more solutions, accompanied by visual demonstrations. Together, these goals, solutions, and demonstrations form a bank of tips and drawing secrets that will increase your graphic proficiency as they improve the quality of your finished pieces.

Custom interiors

As you may recall from the *Applying stroke and fills* section of Chapter 3, fill options vary dramatically from software to software. Near the end of the section, we mentioned that many advanced applications provide a masking feature, which allows you to fill shapes with other filled paths in order to create highly realistic, custom interiors.

Unfortunately, some applications lack masking options. But custom interiors are so utilitarian that it would be a shame for you to think you cannot access them merely because your program has not automated the process. In fact, creating a mask manually is a technique that anyone can master.

Our first tip describes how to fill any shape with a complex, customized interior. We call this tip the cookie-cutter method, because it involves clipping away a collection of paths to match the outline of a shape.

The cookie-cutter method

First draw the shape that you want to fill. You may use any drawing tool, but the path must be closed. We recommend that you keep your shape simple when using this method; complicated forms and complicated interiors generally do not work well together. Stroke the shape with a solid outline and apply a transparent fill. Next, clone the shape and drag the clone to an empty portion of your screen. The clone will serve as both guide and cookie cutter.

Create your custom interior using the outline of the cloned shape as a guide. Feel free to draw outside the lines as much as you want, since any sloppiness can easily be cleaned up later.

Use the cookie-cutter method to cover up excess images around a shape while leaving its custom interior visible.

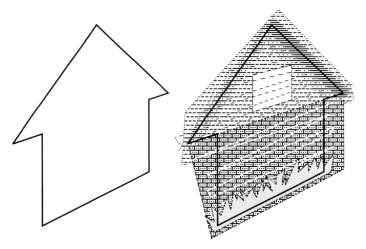

First we created the shape on the left to represent the side of a house. We then cloned the house shape and added a collection of paths behind it. Notice that we have made no attempt to keep the paths within the outline of the house shape. All excess portions will be clipped away in the next step.

The idea of the cookie-cutter method is to cover up the excess images around a shape while leaving its custom interior visible. Therefore, when creating the cookie cutter shape itself, we want to enclose the area outside the shape, while opening up the area inside it.

To create the cookie cutter, you must reshape the cloned image. Select the cloned shape with your software's reshape tool, or select the shape and choose the "Reshape" command. Insert a corner point into a straight segment near the top of the shape, and drag this point to a location directly above the shape. Insert four more corner points and position them to form a rectangle around the image. Insert a sixth corner point and overlap it onto the corner point directly above the shape. And finally, insert a seventh corner point and position it to restore the image to its original appearance. A rectangle will now surround your shape, with a straight line connecting the rectangle to the shape.

Since the rectangle and house are both parts of the same path, it is the area around the house that is now enclosed.

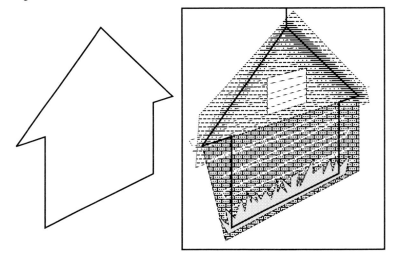

To create our cookie cutter, we inserted seven corner points into the straight segment along the roof and relocated these points to create a rectangle surrounding the house. Since the rectangle and house are both parts of the same path, it is the area around the house that is now enclosed. The area that appears inside the house is empty.

After the cookie cutter is complete, fill it with white and delete its stroke.

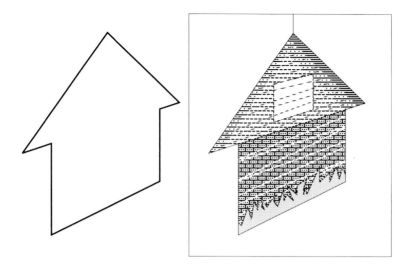

Filling the cookie cutter with white conceals excess images around the masking shape.

By filling the cookie cutter with white, we conceal the excess images around the house. Normally, you will want to delete the stroke entirely, but we have left a thin outline to show the boundaries of the cookie cutter.

The last step is to re-establish the outline of the mask. Your original image should still be set aside. Select this image and drag it directly over the clone.

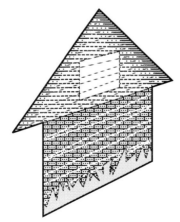

After deleting the stroke from the cookie cutter and dragging the original shape into position, the house mask is complete.

To avoid accidentally jostling one of the many paths that make up your custom interior, you may want to group all paths with the cookie cutter and the original shape. You may then add other paths with standard or transparent fills to produce a finished illustration.

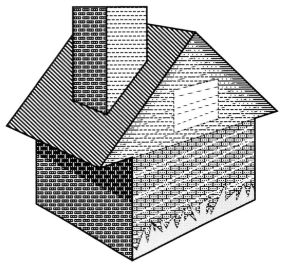

Here we have combined our custom shape with several other paths to produce a finished house. None of these paths may contain a custom interior.

The possibilities for the kinds of custom fills you can create are endless. You will probably want to experiment with using multiple colors, tints, and bitmapped or object-oriented patterns. No matter how wild or detailed you make your custom fill, the cookie-cutter method makes it quick and easy to mask it with a shape to produce dazzling, sophisticated results.

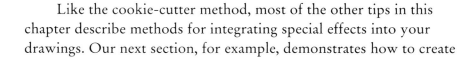

Like the cookie-cutter method, most of the other tips in this chapter describe methods for integrating special effects into your drawings. Our next section, for example, demonstrates how to create custom outlines by applying special line effects. Keep in mind, we do *not* recommend that you apply both a custom interior *and* a custom outline to the same shape. However, you may create interesting images that incorporate line effects as elements inside their custom interiors.

Special line effects

When you stroke a path, you probably consider your alternatives in basic terms: What color or gray value should you use? What's the best line weight? If you're really looking for something different, you might even add dashes.

In most cases, these alternatives are sufficient. But your possibilities do not end here. If you're looking for a unusual way to add excitement and texture to a dull, uninspiring image, you can apply special line effects.

If you want to add excitement and texture to an uninspiring image, you can apply special line effects.

This image is straightforward and obvious, but it lacks flair.

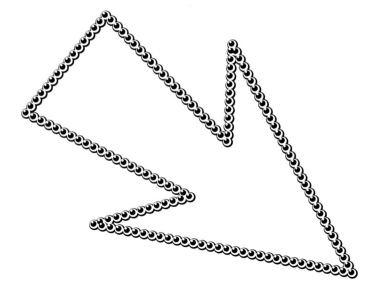

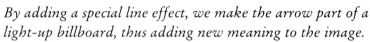

Line effects are created by layering duplicates of an image with slightly different strokes.

By adding a special line effect, we make the arrow part of a light-up billboard, thus adding new meaning to the image.

Line effects adds energy to a drawing without overwhelming it or diminishing its elegant simplicity. Some programs offer an array of special stroking patterns. But if your software does not, you may build a line effect using one of the two methods described in the following paragraphs.

The stroke-on-stroke method

Line effects are created by layering duplicates of an image, one copy in front of another, each with a slightly different stroke. Provided that the line weight of each stroke is thinner than the line weight of the stroke behind it, portions of each stroke will show through to create an "in-line" effect. For example, try stroking a simple image with a black, 10-point line weight. Then copy the image, paste the copy directly in front of the original, and stroke the copy with a white, 8-point line weight. Finally, paste another copy directly in front of the two existing images and stroke it with a black, 4-point line weight. The result will look something like the following figure.

In-line effects are created by layering images that are identical except for slightly different strokes. The line weight of each path should be thinner than the weight of the path behind it. This allows some of each stroke to show through.

In the previous example, we used black and white lines only. By introducing colors or gray values, we expand our capabilities. Try creating a light gray line about 10 points thick. Then paste a slightly thinner, slight darker line in front of that. Continue layering thinner, darker lines, ending with a 1-point, 100% black stroke. The result will be a soft, fading line, as shown below.

Create a gradient stroke effect by layering progressively thinner, darker lines.

This gradient stroke was created by layering progressively thinner, darker lines.

The exposed portions of a thick stroke show up on both sides of the path.

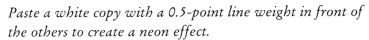

Paste a white copy with a 0.5-point line weight in front of the others to create a neon effect.

Note that all of these effects are created by applying various strokes to images, but no fills. When a thick stroke is placed behind a thinner stroke, portions of the thick stroke show up on both sides of the path. For example, if a path stroked with a white, 4-point line weight covers a path stroked with a black, 6-point line weight, the final image will appear to be surrounded by two 1-point black lines, separated by a 4-point gully. A fill will obstruct those portions of a stroke visible on the inside of a shape. If you want to fill a shape stroked with a special effects outline, add a filled copy of the shape *behind* the stroked copies. An example of this technique is shown in the following tip.

The layer-and-offset method

When you layer a stroked copy directly in front of another, the forward stroke appears centered inside the stroke behind it. Half the exposed portion of the thicker stroke appears on each side of the

Developing a Successful Drawing Technique

thinner stroke. However, if you offset the forward stroke slightly, the rear stroke will appear heavier on one side, creating a three-dimensional effect.

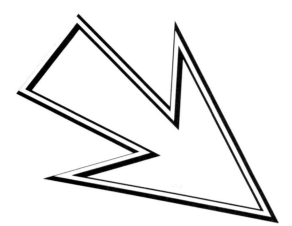

Use the layer-and-offset method to produce three-dimensional images that appear raised from the page.

We stroked the arrow shape with a black, 10-point line weight. We then cloned the shape, applied a white, 4-point stroke, and moved it two points upward and two points to the left. The resulting image appears slightly raised off the page.

Unfortunately, the layer-and-offset method produces less predictable results than the straightforward stroke-on-stroke method. In several portions of the figure above, the white outline comes close to touching the white background. Exactly where it touches is almost impossible to anticipate in advance of creating the image. You may use this inexact method to achieve subtle effects in which the invisible and visible portions of an image share almost equal influence. But as a beginning artist, you may prefer to clearly distinguish the foreground of an image from its background by introducing a fill, as demonstrated in the figure at the top of the next page.

To fill a path stroked with a special-effect outline, add a filled copy of the path behind the stroked copies.

To better distinguish an offset stroke from the area around it, you may add a fill behind your strokes. Here we have pasted a path filled with a gradation in back of the two stroked paths.

When applied to curves, the layer-and-offset method can be used to create calligraphic lines and shapes.

Even random squiggles can be elevated to high-relief callig-raphy using the layer-and-offset method.

So far, we have combined multiple strokes to create various solid-line images. But none of these bear much resemblance to the ornate figure shown at the beginning of the *Special line effects* section.

To create lines that look like checkered paths or strings of beads, we must combine what we have learned so far with the stroke attributes of cap and dash pattern.

The caps-and-dashes method

This tip is especially designed to be used by owners of drawing programs that offer both cap options and editable dash patterns. If your program lacks these functions, you will be able to approximate some of our sample images, but you won't be able to emulate them exactly.

In Chapter 3, we discussed how caps affect the beginning and ending of each dash in a dash pattern. The caps-and-dashes method merely builds on this principle. If you layer identical paths that have similar caps and dash patterns but different line weights and colors, you can create hollow dashes and dashes within dashes, as demonstrated in the following figures.

You may use the caps-and-dashes method if your program offers both cap options and editable dash patterns.

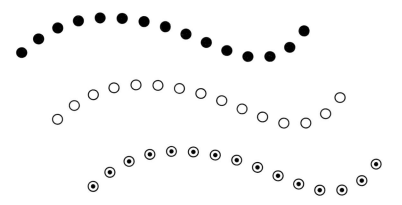

In the first line, we have applied a 10-point line weight with round caps and a dash pattern with 0-point dashes and 20-point gaps. To create the second image, we have cloned the line and stroked it with a white, 8-point line weight. The caps and dash pattern are left unchanged. In the third image, we have cloned the second line and used a black, 4-point line weight.

This method works by establishing a constant dash pattern and varying the line weight, color, and caps.

These images are identical to the ones in the previous figure, except that we have applied square caps instead of round.

When using the caps-and-dashes method, you generally establish a constant dash pattern and vary only the line weight and color of the layered paths. To create squares inside of circles or vice versa, you may switch back and forth between round and square caps.

If your software doesn't provide caps options, but does allow you to edit dash patterns, you may create interesting effects by varying a dash pattern from path to path.

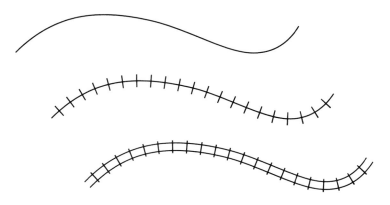

In the first image, we have a solid 1-point line. We have then added a clone with a 12-point line weight and a dash pattern of 1-point dashes and 12-point gaps. The result is a stitch

effect. In the third image, we have assigned the rear path a 10-point line weight, covered with an 8-point white clone to create the train-track line effect.

To create the light-up billboard effect shown at the beginning of this section, we combined four paths with round caps and tight dash patterns. We then offset each path slightly to create a highlight effect.

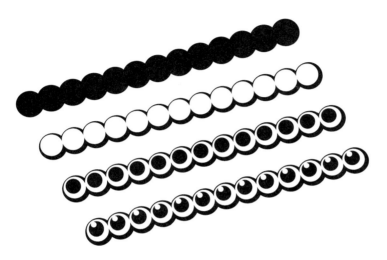

You may offset layered paths stroked with dash patterns to create a highlight effect.

By enlarging the line effect shown in the introduction to this section, we can examine how each path was added. The effect combines principles from the caps-and-dashes method with those of the layer-and-offset method.

A note of warning: Keep in mind that line effects become less predictable as they become more complex. This is especially true if your path has any corner points, because every line effect composed of a dash pattern has its own rhythm, determined by the length of each dash and gap. If the rhythm of the line doesn't coincide with the length of a segment, two segments may appear to meet awkwardly at a corner.

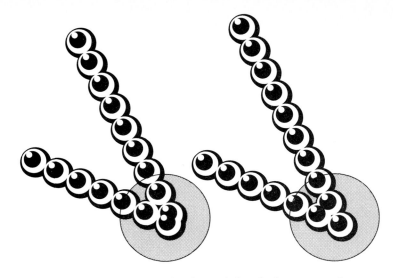

If the rhythm of a dash pattern doesn't coincide with the length of a segment, the effect muddles at the corner point.

In the left example, the rhythm of the dash pattern does not coincide with the length of each segment, creating a sort of double yoke effect at the corner point. When using complex line effects, this is the case more often than not. By experimenting with the placement of the corner point, we eventually align it with the dash pattern, as shown on the right.

If you're looking for a precise means of eliminating corner point problems, you can try to match the length of the segment to the rhythm of the dash pattern. For example, if your dash pattern is made up of 4-point dashes and 8-point gaps, the pattern repeats every 12 points. If the length of every segment in a path is a whole-number multiple of this 12-point rhythm, the line effect will meet each corner point exactly.

Unfortunately, you can measure only straight segments with any degree of accuracy. If your path includes curved segments, you will have to experiment with the positions of your corner points.

Together, the stroke-on-stroke, layer-and-offset, and caps-and-dashes methods offer so many possibilities that we can't begin to

Developing a Successful Drawing Technique

demonstrate all of them. We do hope that you have gained sufficient insight from these brief discussions and figures to experiment and discover your own line effects that will brighten up otherwise common images.

Adding a shadow to an image

Shadows enhance the realism of your drawing and imply the nature of an object's environment.

In real life, everything has a shadow. It doesn't matter whether it's noon, the sun is setting, you're indoors and the only light source is a small window, or you're on a lonely road at midnight under a street lamp; every object always has a shadow. You can choose to ignore shadows in your drawings, but adding a shadow invariably enhances the realism of any image. Shadows also provide information about an object's environment. For example, if an object and its shadow touch, then the object is touching some surface—presumably the ground—at that point. If the object and its shadow do not touch, then the object is hovering above the surface upon which the shadow is cast.

The shape of a shadow is dependent on the form of the object that casts it. This makes shadows very difficult to draw accurately with a pencil on paper. But using a computer, it's much easier, because a shadow is simply a transformed clone.

The fill-scale-and-skew method

To create a shadow, you must first clone the image that casts it. Select all paths that make up the image and drag clones of these paths to an empty portion of your page. Shadows are not as detailed as the objects that cast them; in fact, they have no detail whatsoever except their outlines. Therefore, while your clones are still selected, fill them with a light gray and apply no stroke. This will obliterate all detail inside the cloned image and leave you with an exact outline.

Although this hockey player is an extremely complex image, it will be easy for us to give it an accurate shadow. A shadow increases the realism of the graphic and offers hints about the athlete's environment.

You may change an image to a silhouette simply by filling all paths with a light gray and choosing no stroke.

After cloning all paths that make up the hockey player, we change the clone into a silhouette by filling all its paths with a light gray and choosing no stroke. In general, the image

Developing a Successful Drawing Technique

looks great; however, it has a few inaccuracies. The area below the athlete's raised left arm as well as the area between his right leg and his stick should be white, since light would be able to pass through these areas. Also, the sock lines on his left leg should be filled in, since light cannot pass through these areas.

After making the lighted areas white and filling in the solid areas, we end up with this accurate silhouette. We have included a vertical line to the right of the athlete indicating his height for comparison with the following figure.

After fine-tuning your silhouette, delete any unnecessary paths to minimize the size of your file.

After fine-tuning your silhouette, you may want to remove any unnecessary paths that do not contribute to the overall outline. Then select all paths in the silhouette and choose the "Group" command.

The next step is optional, depending on whether you want to cast your shadow in front of or behind the image itself. A shadow is cast by an object onto the ground below it. When you are translating the three dimensions of real life onto the two dimensions of a piece of paper, the portion of the ground that is in front of an image is represented fully below the image and the portion behind the image starts at the base of the image and extend upward and behind the image on the paper. This is because the ground appears to recede upward toward your visual horizon, as described in the *Demonstrating depth* section of Chapter 2.

The practical application of these facts is that if you plan to position a shadow in front of your object, you must flip it vertically before going any farther. You can accomplish this either by choosing a "Flip vertical" command or by dragging the one of the top corner transformation handles downward past the lower transformation handles. However, if you want to create a shadow behind the image, do not flip your silhouette.

The next two operations—scaling and skewing—must be performed, but the amount of either of these operations is entirely up to you. Generally, you will need to reduce a shadow vertically to indicate that the light source is above the image. If you enlarge your shadow, the light source must be very low, like a setting sun. Do not, however, reduce or enlarge the horizontal proportions of your shadow. Then, while the shadow is still selected, choose the "Slant" or "Skew" command and drag the top or bottom handle either left or right, so that the shadow slants away from the light source.

If you plan to position a shadow in front of an image, you must flip your silhouette vertically.

We'll position our shadow in front of the hockey player, so we have flipped our silhouette vertically. We have also scaled and skewed the shadow, as echoed by the line to the right of the shadow. Notice that the line is shorter than the vertical line in the previous figure, indicating that the shadow has been reduced vertically. The line is also slanted about 45°, indicating that we have skewed the shadow dramatically rightward.

After the shadow is finished, it should be coupled with the image itself. If the shadow is behind the image, the shadow should be sent to back. If the image touches the ground or some other surface, the image and shadow should touch. If the image is hovering or in flight, its shadow should not touch the image.

To make an image appear to touch the ground, position the shadow so that it just touches the image.

We next place the shadow below the hockey player to indicate that the light source is in back of him. Notice that the athlete touches his shadow daintily with one foot, as if he is just beginning to leap.

Unless an image is standing on a perfectly horizontal surface, your shadow will not touch at all appropriate points. In the preceding figure, for example, the hockey player's left foot touches the shadow, but his right foot appears to hang in the air. If you want to make him appear to be standing with both feet on the ground, you must skew the shadow vertically. Some reshaping may also be required.

When an image appears three-dimensional, its shadow may need to be skewed vertically and reshaped.

To set the hockey player's right foot on the ground, we have skewed the shadow vertically. The horizontal lines in the marker to the right demonstrate the angle of our skew. Unfortunately, this skewing caused the hockey stick's shadow to extend past the stick itself, creating a very unnatural effect. We have reshaped the shadow slightly to turn it into the finished drawing shown above.

Developing a Successful Drawing Technique

If you want to further enhance your image, fill your shadow with a gradation. The shadow should be darkest at the point closest to the image, since this area has the least possibility for reflected light. From this point, the shadow fades (and lightens) outward.

— · ✦ ◆ ✦ · —

A shadow can add realism to the simplest or the most complex object. Not only is it easy to create, but a shadow can serve more than one purpose: it indicates the location and nature of your light source and tells the audience where the ground is in relationship to an image. The best thing about the fill-scale-and-skew method is that it permits you to add sophistication to a graphic—such as a piece of clip-art—even if you have little or no drawing technique.

Type effects

Our next collection of tips explore ways to manipulate type in a drawing program. In general, type is treated similarly to other graphic elements. All drawing programs allow you to fill text with a color. Most programs allow you to stroke text with a specific line weight and color. A few high-end programs even let you join type to a free-form path. This section explains how to use filled text, stroked text, and text on a curve to achieve a variety of special type effects.

Filling effects

The most simple text effect you can create in a drawing program is the drop shadow. A drop shadow makes a block of text appear to be raised above the page, casting its shadow evenly on the surface of the paper. To create a drop shadow, clone a block of text and fill the clone

This section explains how to use filled text, stroked text, and text on a curve.

with a light tint. Something comparable to a 30% black tint generally works best, but a solid light color such as cyan or magenta is also acceptable. Move the clone a few points down and to the side of the original text block, then layer the clone behind the original.

Drop Shadow

To create this drop shadow, we moved the clone just two points down and to the right of the original. This way, the text appears to barely hover above the page. The result is a very legible block of special-effect type.

Moving a shadow away from its text block creates a more pronounced effect but reduces legibility.

Drop Shadow

As you move a shadow farther from the original, the drop shadow effect becomes more pronounced, but the text becomes less legible as well.

Developing a Successful Drawing Technique

A single drop shadow raises your text from the page. If you're looking for something a little more exciting, multiple drop shadows can be used with multiple blocks of type to add the appearance of motion to your type. In the following figure, we have set multiple drop shadows against a black background to produce the effect of type moving toward the viewer. We start with four lines of type, created using different styles and type sizes, and filled with a 97% black tint. Next, we clone the text block, enlarge it to 105% of its previous size, and fill it with the slightly lighter shade of 94% black. We then clone this text block, enlarge it to 105%, and fill it with a black tint that is 3% lighter (91% black). We repeat this process several times. We fill the final text block with solid white, to clearly distinguish it from the drop shadows behind it.

Multiple drop shadows can be combined with multiple lines of text to create the effect of type rushing toward the viewer.

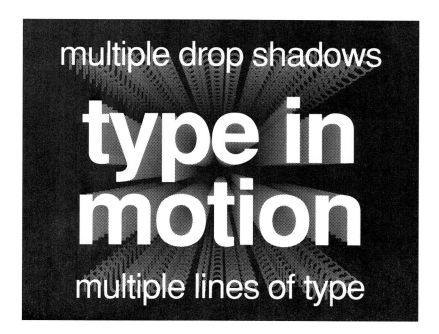

This image contains 18 drop shadows, each of which is filled with a black tint that is 3% lighter than the text block immediately behind it. The foremost drop shadow is filled with a 46% black tint, which permits the white type to stand out clearly.

Drop shadows are not the only shadow effect you can create using filled type. You can also create shadows using the fill-scale-and-skew method described in the previous section.

To create this image, we merely cloned the text block, flipped it horizontally, and filled it with a medium gray value (a tint of black). We then sent the clone behind the original text block to prevent any gray letters from partially overlapping the black characters. To complete the effect, we created a light gray box behind both text blocks.

Clone a text block and flip it vertically to make a reflection; skew it to make a shadow.

The greatest difference between this image and the previous figure is that we have skewed the clone to make it look more like a shadow and less like a reflection. The nice thing about an angled shadow is that you can layer body text over it, as we have done here. For example, a headline can appear as if it is casting a shadow over the text below it.

Developing a Successful Drawing Technique

Incidentally, you cannot apply skewed shadows to text blocks that contain a lowercase *g*, *p*, or other letter with a descender. In a shadow, a descender would extend past the letter that cast it, creating an unrealistic effect. If you must use *g* or *p* in a block of shadow text, we recommend that you use capital letters only.

Stroking effects

If your software allows you to stroke type, then several more text effects options are available to you. These include any of the special line-effect methods described earlier in this chapter.

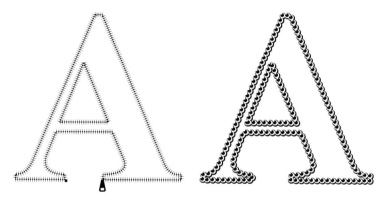

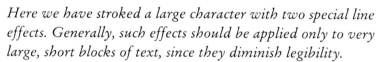

In many drawing programs, a special line effect can be applied to type.

Here we have stroked a large character with two special line effects. Generally, such effects should be applied only to very large, short blocks of text, since they diminish legibility.

Not all stroking effects require this much effort. In fact, one of the simplest stroking techniques is one of the most effective. By layering a filled text block in front of a stroked drop shadow, you may make type appear raised or sunken. To make text appear raised, first fill the text block with white. Then clone the text block and stroke the clone with a heavy dark outline. Move the clone down and to the right a distance equal to half its line weight. Then send it behind the original.

Type may be
made to appear
raised or sunken
by positioning
it in front
of a dark,
stroked clone.

Raised type

Type appears raised when filled with light value and offset slightly in front of a dark, stroked clone. Raised type adds texture to a drawing.

You may create sunken type in the same way, except that instead of filling the forward text block with white, use a light tint. And instead of offsetting the drop shadow down and to the right, move it up and to the left.

Sunken type

Type appears sunken when filled with a light tint and offset slightly in front of a dark, stroked clone. The effect isn't perfect, because the forward text block covers interior portions of letters—such as "o" and "e"—that would show through if the type were truly carved into stone.

Developing a Successful Drawing Technique

Sunken type

If your drawing program allows you to mask other elements with type, you may create a different kind of sunken text by masking the forward text block with the drop shadow type. As you can see above, masked text tends to look more like it was cut out of paper than carved into stone.

Our last stroking effect is applicable specifically to type. It is simply this: stroke text with an outline that matches the color of the fill to create a heavier, or bolder version of a font. This is a fairly obvious technique, and one that is used quite commonly. However, did you know that you can also make type lighter using stroke? Because half the thickness of a line weight rides on the inside of a letter, type may be made lighter by applying a white stroke. An example of this is shown on the following page.

When creating stroked text effects, you should be aware that the way a stroked block of type looks on screen probably does not match the way it will look when printed. Because one of the intentions of a font is to save disk and memory space, its screen representation is usually only a crude approximation of its printed appearance. And even when the font displays perfectly on screen, most programs do not display stroking effects correctly.

The way a stroked block of type looks on your screen probably does not match the way it will look when printed.

Normal
Heavy
Light

Type appears
lighter when
stroked with a
thin, white
outline.

Shown above is a block of Helvetica type as it appears with no stroke, a 3-point black stroke, and a 2-point white stroke. A thick line weight will produce the most noticeable results, but it may also corrupt the delicate proportions of some letters. Stick with thin line weights whenever possible.

Text on a spiral

We've all seen text on a curve, and many of us have even experimented with it. If you own a high-end drawing program that accommodates text with a free-form baseline, you probably know that setting text on a curve is fairly easy, but controlling how and where your type is positioned along the path can be substantially more difficult.

Text always begins at the first point in a path. If you draw a path from left to right, the left point will be the first point and the right point will be the last point. Text will adhere to such a path right-side up. However, if you draw a path from right to left, the right point will

Developing a Successful Drawing Technique

be first and the left point will be last. Since text never follows a path backward, it must appear upside-down. If your text appears upside-down after fitting it to a curve, undo the text fitting command, flip the path horizontally, and try again. Flipping a path horizontally sends the beginning and ending points to opposite sides of the path.

But what do you do if your beginning and ending points are not on the left and right sides of a path, but on the inside and the outside, as in the case of a spiral? Currently, no software offers a command that turns a path inside out.

To create text on a spiral, you must create your path correctly in the first place. This tip explains how to create spirals that not only progress in the correct direction, but also look fluid and precise.

The first step is to draw a large circle, four to five inches in diameter. Then ungroup the circle or convert it to curves, depending on your software. The circle is now an editable path.

A spiral is similar to a series of concentric circles. To create type that spirals inward, your concentric circles must start from the outside, and progress inward. Therefore, each of following circles you create must be smaller than the existing one. Clone your circle an reduce it to 90%. If your software offers such controls, be sure to scale the circle with reference to its center. Now clone your *original* circle again (not the clone), and scale it to 80%. Repeatedly cloning and scaling your original circle provides a consistent distance between one circle and the next.

Continue to clone your original circle and reduce it to a size 10% smaller than the previous reduction. Clone the original circle nine times—this last, innermost circle will be reduced to 10%.

If your text appears upside-down when fit to a curve, undo the text fitting command, flip the path horizontally, and try again.

A spiral can be based on a series of concentric circles.

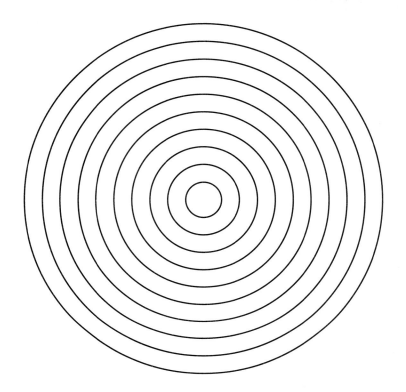

The first step in drawing a spiral is to create a series of ten concentric circles, each one spaced an equal distance between each of its neighbors.

Now split each circle into two halves by breaking apart the 3 o'clock and 9 o'clock (right and left) points in each shape. In most software, this is accomplished using a special reshaping tool in combination with a "Split" or "Break" command.

After splitting your circles into 20 semicircles, select all the bottom halves and move them directly to the right until the left point in the outermost bottom half meets the left point in the second-to-outermost top half. All other points will line up as shown in the following figure.

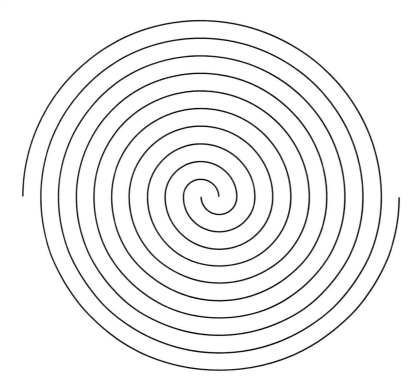

Split the circles in half and drag the bottom halves one increment to the right.

By nudging the bottom halves one concentric increment to the right, you create a pattern of two spirals, intertwined like coils in a spring.

Join all overlapping points. This is generally accomplished by marqueeing the points with the reshape tool or the arrow tool and choosing a "Join" command. In some software, you must first combine the semicircles before joining their points.

You now have two complete spirals. If you want, you may use both of them to create the effect of two blocks of text woven together. Or you may connect the two innermost points to force a single block of text to spiral inward and then spiral back out. However, in most cases, you will simply want to choose between the two and delete the one you don't want.

Now fit your text to the path. The text will start at the outermost point in the spiral and progress inward. Depending on font and type size, a spiral can accommodate about four sentences of text.

To make text spiral outward, start with a small circle and enlarge it to create your spiral.

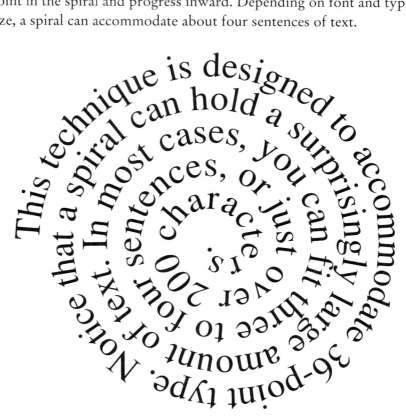

This sample spiraling text block contains about 200 letters.

Several variations on this technique are possible. If you want to fit more type on your spiral at a smaller point size, reduce your cloned circles in increments of 5% rather than 10%. If you want to use a smaller quantity of large type, reduce your circles in 20% increments. If you want to create text that spirals outward instead of inward, start with a small circle and enlarge it in 10% increments, starting at 110%.

Type is more easily manipulated in a drawing program than in any other kind of software. It can be filled or stroked to create any number of special effects. It can also be fixed to a free-form or geometric path. It can even be filled, stroked, *and* joined to a path.

Throughout your type manipulations, always try to keep in mind that the ultimate purpose of type is to be read. If you alter it so much that it becomes illegible, then you have most certainly gone too far. As a test, you may want to show your special type effects to a couple of friends. If they squint and struggle to piece together individual syllables, then you know that your style has overwhelmed your content.

Creating seamless gradations

Our final tip addresses how to create consistent shading effects using gradations. Unlike other tips in this chapter, this gradation tip does not work in every drawing program. In fact, it is applicable only to the select few that offer a blending feature. So, consider it a bonus. While not essential, it should prove very helpful to skilled users with advanced software.

Gradations are transitional fills in which one gray value or color fades into another gray value or color through a series of incremental tints, known as *steps*. In Chapter 3, we introduced the concept of gradations, and mentioned that some drawing programs provide automated gradation features. Such features tend to be limiting, not allowing you to determine the exact shape of beginning and ending steps.

Gradations are transitional fills in which one color fades into another through a series of incremental steps.

Blending differently colored paths

If your software provides a *blending* feature, you can create custom gradations. In a custom gradation, you determine not only the shape of each step, but also the number of steps and even the color of each step. Creating a custom gradation requires more work, but allows the user more control and, as a result, makes it possible to produce more realistic shading effects.

To create a custom gradation, select two paths that have an identical number of points but differently colored fills. Then invoke the blend feature, as instructed in your owner's manual. A dialog box will appear, requesting the number of steps you want to create. Enter a number and press the return key to begin the blending operation. Each step is created as a separate path with a unique fill.

Your software's blending feature allows you to create custom gradations.

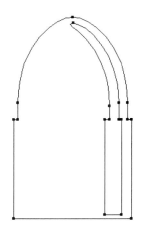

On the left, we have selected two paths. Imagine that the interior path is white and the outer path is black. After invoking the blend feature and requesting 98 steps, our program creates a series of 98 incremental paths, each filled with a unique gray value. The result is a smooth, custom gradation, as shown on the right.

You will probably need to experiment with this feature a few times to fully master the procedure. If your steps turn out to be shaped differently than you had expected, it may be because your original paths contain a dissimilar number of points or because you have selected unlike points in the paths.

Generally, however, the problems that appear when you print your drawing are the most difficult ones to predict. Rather than being a seamless gradation, your gradation may display a distinct *banding* effect, wherein every step appears distinct from its neighbors.

A gradation with too few or too many steps displays distinct bands, often inconsistent in size.

Banding results when a custom gradation contains too few or too many steps. Here, the banding is very pronounced, because we have used only eleven steps.

To avoid banding, you must use a sufficient number of steps so that each step is small enough to go unnoticed. For best results, each step should be about one point wide, or about 72 steps per inch. Also, the size of steps should be consistent. Although your software automatically creates consistently sized steps, each step may not correspond to a unique gray value in your printer. Two neighboring steps printed with the same gray value will look like one unusually large step.

How can you make sure a step is going to correspond to a unique gray value in your printer? To answer this question, we must examine some principles of gray value theory.

Gray value theory

Every printer is capable of printing a specific number of gray values, depending on its *resolution* (the number of pixels it prints per inch) and its *screen frequency* (the number of halftone dots it prints per inch). Resolution is typically measured in dots per inch, or *dpi*. Frequency is measured in lines per inch, or *lpi*. The resolution of your printer is often fixed, but the screen frequency can always be changed. For example, a standard laser printer prints 300 dpi, regardless of your software. While the default screen frequency for a laser printer is 60 lpi, some drawing programs allow you to alter this number.

Since a setting of 60 lpi assigns 60 halftone dots per inch, every halftone cell printed on a 300-dpi laser printer measures five pixels wide by five pixels tall (300 ÷ 60 = 5), for a total of 25 pixels. If all pixels are turned off, the halftone cell appears white, all pixels turned on produces black, and any number between 0 and 25 produces a shade of gray. A unique tint can be created by turning on each of 0 through 25 pixels, for a total of 26 gray values.

To determine the maximum number of gray value producible by any printer, use the following formula:

The maximum number of steps in a gradation depends on the resolution and screen frequency of your printer.

$$\left(\mathrm{dpi}\middle/\mathrm{lpi}\right)^2 + 1 = \text{\textit{maximum number of gray values}}$$

The standard number of gray values producible by a Linotronic 100 imagesetter is $(1270 \div 90)^2 + 1 \approx 200$. For the higher-resolution L300, the number of gray values is $(2540 \div 120)^2 + 1 \approx 448$. Unfortunately, the PostScript language can describe only 256 gray values, regardless of printer resolution. So the actual maximum number of gray values producible by an L300 must be a whole number that is (a) a multiple of 448 and (b) less than 256, such as 448 ÷ 2 = 224.

Percentage change in color

If you want to print a gradation between solid black and solid white to a 1270-dpi imagesetter, you should create 198 steps; that is, 200 gray values minus back and white themselves. The result will be an extremely smooth gradation with as little banding as possible. But what if you want to create a smaller gradation, say from a 30% red tint to a 70% red tint? Simply subtract the lighter tint value from the darker tint to determine the percentage change in color. Multiply this percentage change by the total number of gray values and subtract 2 to allow for the beginning and ending tints themselves.

Therefore, the revised formula is as follows:

$$\left(\left(^{\text{dpi}}\!/_{\text{lpi}}\right)^{2}+1\right) \times \%^{\,change}_{\,in\ color} - 2 = {optimal\ number \atop of\ steps}$$

If the (dpi ÷ lpi)² + 1 expression is greater than 256, you should divide it by 2 before multiplying it by the percentage change in color.

Size of gradation

So far, the only variable we have neglected to take into account is the size of the gradation. Many gradations are small. If your gradation covers only half an inch, there's no sense is using 198 steps, each of which is thinner than your fingernail. In fact, you should never use more steps in a single inch than there are halftone cells. Generally, the best rule of thumb is to use about one step per point, or 72 steps per inch, as we mentioned earlier.

There is no need to include more steps in an inch of gradation than there are halftone cells.

The following five tables are designed to help you determine the number of steps to use in a custom gradation. They account for producible gray values, percentage change, and length of gradation. They also figure in the PostScript-language limit of 256 gray values. Locate the table that matches your printer's resolution and screen frequency. This should be the printer you will use for final output, not your proofing printer. Notice that no printer with a resolution of less than 1270 dpi is listed, eliminating all laser printers and lesser devices. Quite frankly, it almost impossible to produce a smooth gradation on a printer that cannot produce at least 100 gray values, regardless of mathematical accuracy of your blend. We recommend that you always use an imagesetter for final output of gradations. If you do not know which table to use, contact your service bureau.

After you locate the correct table, find the length of the gradation listed along the top that is equal to or longer than the length of your blend, and match this value with the percentage change listed along the side. The corresponding number in the grid is the number of steps you should enter into your software's blending dialog box.

Consult the table that matches the printer you'll be using for final output.

1270 dpi, 90 lpi

Length of gradation

Inches	0.25	0.50	0.75	1.00	1.50	2.00	3.00
Points	**18**	**36**	**54**	**72**	**108**	**144**	**216**
10%	18	18	18	18	18	18	18
20%	18	38	38	38	38	38	38
30%	18	28	58	58	58	58	58
40%	18	38	38	78	78	78	78
50%	18	31	48	48	98	98	98
60%	18	38	58	58	58	118	118
70%	18	33	45	68	68	138	138
80%	18	38	51	78	78	78	158
90%	18	34	58	58	88	88	178
100%	18	38	48	65	98	98	198

Percentage change in color

1270 dpi, 120 lpi

Length of gradation

Inches	0.25	0.50	0.75	1.00	1.50	2.00	3.00
Points	18	36	54	72	108	144	216
10%	9	9	9	9	9	9	9
20%	21	21	21	21	21	21	21
30%	15	32	32	32	32	32	32
40%	21	21	43	43	43	43	43
50%	17	26	55	55	55	55	55
60%	21	32	32	66	66	66	66
70%	18	38	38	77	77	77	77
80%	21	28	43	43	88	88	88
90%	18	32	49	49	100	100	100
100%	21	36	55	55	111	111	111

Percentage change in color

All tables take into account maximum gray values producible, percentage change, and length of gradation.

2540 dpi, 120 lpi

Length of gradation

Inches	0.25	0.50	0.75	1.00	1.50	2.00	3.00
Points	18	36	54	72	108	144	216
10%	20	43	43	43	43	43	43
20%	20	43	43	43	88	88	88
30%	20	43	43	65	133	133	133
40%	20	43	58	58	88	88	178
50%	20	43	54	73	110	110	223
60%	20	43	52	65	88	133	133
70%	20	43	50	77	103	103	155
80%	20	43	58	70	88	118	178
90%	20	43	56	79	99	133	200
100%	20	43	54	73	110	148	223

Percentage change in color

2540 dpi, 133 lpi

Length of gradation

Inches	0.25	0.50	0.75	1.00	1.50	2.00	3.00
Points	**18**	**36**	**54**	**72**	**108**	**144**	**216**
10%	16	35	35	35	35	35	35
20%	22	35	35	71	71	71	71
30%	20	35	53	53	108	108	108
40%	22	35	47	71	71	144	144
50%	21	35	59	59	89	89	181
60%	22	35	53	71	108	108	217
70%	21	35	49	62	83	126	126
80%	22	35	57	71	96	144	144
90%	22	35	53	80	108	108	163
100%	21	35	59	71	89	120	181

Percentage change in color

2540 dpi, 150 lpi

Length of gradation

Inches	0.25	0.50	0.75	1.00	1.50	2.00	3.00
Points	**18**	**36**	**54**	**72**	**108**	**144**	**216**
10%	12	27	27	27	27	27	27
20%	17	27	56	56	56	56	56
30%	20	27	41	41	84	84	84
40%	21	36	56	56	113	113	113
50%	19	34	46	70	70	142	142
60%	20	33	56	56	84	84	171
70%	20	38	48	65	99	99	199
80%	21	36	56	75	113	113	228
90%	20	35	50	63	84	127	127
100%	20	34	56	70	94	142	142

Percentage change in color

Note to service bureaus: The information contained in this tip partially contradicts Adobe's *Colophon 6* article, which does not take into account the PostScript language 256-gray-value maximum, as well as the December 1989 *LaserLetter* article, which recommends always changing your imagesetter's screen frequency, despite the fact that "the imagesetter substitutes its closest possible screen, which can vary from your specification by 10 lpi or more." The preceding tables take into account standardized screen frequencies, PostScript limitations, and the relative sizes of steps and halftone cells.

———◆—●●—◆———

The tips in this chapter have outlined methods for improving the appearance of your images and creating pleasing special effects. Applying these methods in real drawing situations will help you to easily improve the appearance of your finished illustrations and to save time in the bargain. And in using our methods, you will no doubt discover methods of your own, that will increase your proficiency and speed.

In the chapters that follow, we will take you from beginning to end through the creation of some actual illustrations. Occasionally, the concepts we have discussed in this chapter will pop up in both familiar and startlingly different situations. We hope that this background will increase your learning potential and make future projects easier.

Applying Your Knowledge

Basic Hands-On Projects

CHAPTER 5

Now that we have discussed the fundamental techniques, tools, and commands useful in creating any graphic in a drawing program, it is time to work through a series of sample projects. In this chapter and the two that follow, we discuss each of the features and methods that we have introduced so far by actually putting them to use. Each project is "hands-on," demonstrating how to create free-form computer artwork according to easy-to-follow, concise guidelines.

In this chapter, we will create two very basic graphics: a page ornament and a simple cartoon. Each project concentrates on the most elementary aspects of graphic composition. You will learn not only how to think through a illustration, but also how to execute it using a typical drawing application. If at any point you are unsure of a command or tool that we ask you to access, refer to Chapter 3 for a complete discussion.

As you work through each project, don't worry if your graphics do not exactly match ours dot-for-dot. In fact, it is preferable that you work your own style into each project. By following our directions in a manner that seems comfortable to you, you may develop personal drawing habits that will be helpful when you create artwork in the future.

Incidentally, many of the figures in Chapters 5 through 7 do not display strokes and fills. This is because we are viewing these figures in the *key line* (or *wireframe*) display mode, which is available in most drawing programs by turning off the "Preview" command. If your software does not offer such a key line display mode, don't worry; it won't affect your ability to complete the project. It merely allows us to more easily examine the creation and manipulation of paths.

Creating a page ornament

Our first project is to create a page ornament, which is a simplified representation of an everyday object, designed to impart basic information in an immediate and friendly manner. The page ornament we create will be an ordinary house with a tree and a fence.

Our first sample project is to create this easily recognizable picture of a house.

With their immediacy and simplicity, page ornaments can satisfy a number of graphic requirements. Generally, a page ornament is used:

1. to enliven a dull page with little effort.

2. to act as a visual signpost for your reader, highlighting pertinent text.

3. to form a more complex graphic in combination with other page ornaments.

For example, suppose that you need to create a newsletter in a short period of time. You want to be able to throw it together, but you don't want to disappoint your readers with its dull appearance. It doesn't have to be fancy, but it should be visually interesting enough to attract readers and highlight important articles. Page ornaments are perfect for this situation, since they are quick and easy to create. They are also generic enough to be used over and over again, from one newsletter to another, or even multiple times within the same newsletter.

The tool that we will be using to create most of our page ornament is the line tool. The line tool is extremely versatile for creating geometric objects. We will be using this tool first to sketch our shape, and later to add finishing touches.

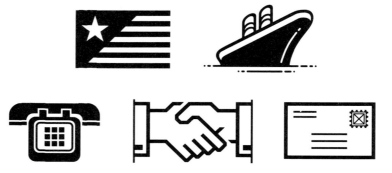

Above are more examples of page ornaments. Each graphic is intuitive; no text is required to explain its purpose or what it represents. Instead, the ornament clarifies and highlights text.

A common mistake when creating a graphic is to start drawing without first establishing some guidelines. For example, we could start drawing at the bottom corner of the tree, then draw the house, then draw its roof, then draw the fence, and so on. This kind of haphazard technique might work well enough to get you through this project, but as you attempt more difficult projects, you will have to spend more and more time reshaping images, transforming images, or deleting images and starting over. If you are sufficiently organized in the first place, you can work through even a complex drawing with only minimal reshaping and redrawing. And the best way to learn efficient drawing habits is to create a simple image, such as a page ornament, deliberately and systematically.

Often, the best plan is to begin by sketching the form of the central object, and then work outward. With this in mind, we will create a simple cross to represent the center of the basic form of the house. We will then use this cross as a reference to create the outline of the house.

Select the line tool from your application toolbox. Then press the shift key and draw a horizontal line the length shown in the following figure. In most programs, you constrain your line to be either horizontal, vertical, or diagonal by pressing the shift key.

Next, press the shift key again, and draw a vertical line that intersects the horizontal line as shown in the figure.

This is the cross created by drawing perpendicular lines with the line tool.

If your software does not offer a line tool, use the polygon or Bézier curve tool to create the lines shown above. For example, to create the horizontal line, click to establish the left point, then shift-click to create the right point and draw a straight line between them.

Now select the rectangle tool. We will use this tool to create the body of the house.

To create the body of the house, draw a rectangle flush underneath the horizontal line, as shown in the following figure. The rectangle should be roughly half again as wide as it is tall, and centered about the vertical line. If you do not draw the shape in exactly the correct position, you may easily move it by dragging it with the arrow tool.

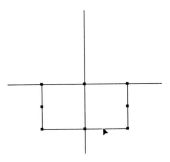

Draw a rectangle extending downward from the horizontal line and centered about the vertical line. If the rectangle isn't exactly aligned on the cross, move it into position after drawing the shape.

Next, select the polygon or Bézier curve tool. We will use this tool to create the roof of the house. Since the roof is made up of two identically sloping sides and a flat, horizontal bottom, a grid will be helpful in ensuring that the shape is symmetrical. If your software offers a grid feature, turn it on now. You may want to set the grid to about 1/16 inch, or 5 points.

Position your cursor on the horizontal line about 1/8 inch to the left of the rectangle, and click. Then press the shift key and click on the vertical line, about 3/4 inch above the horizontal line. A diagonal line will be created between the two points. While still pressing shift, click again on the horizontal line, this time about 1/8 inch to the right of the rectangle. Finally, click on the first point in the shape to complete the triangular roof.

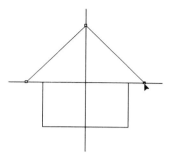

Create the triangular roof by shift-clicking with the polygon or Bézier curve tool. If possible, use a grid to ensure that the shape is symmetrical.

Our next shape will represent the doorway of the house. Select the rectangle tool and draw a thin rectangle overlapping the bottom side of the body of the house, and centered about the vertical line of the cross. If necessary, adjust the positioning of the doorway by dragging it with the arrow tool.

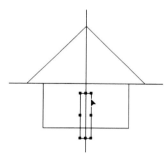

Draw a tall, thin rectangle that extends below the bottom of the house, as shown above. If the rectangle isn't exactly centered on the vertical line, move it into position after drawing the shape.

Next we will create two windows. Since both windows are the same shape and size, we can draw one of them and clone it to create the other. Using the rectangle tool, draw a window inside the left half of the house. It should be a little wider and shorter than the doorway. However, the exact size or position is not important.

To ensure that the second window is symmetrical to the first, we will flip the rectangle with respect to the vertical line of the cross. Using the arrow tool, click on the window and shift-click on the vertical line to select both objects. Now clone them, as described in Chapter 3. If your software lacks a cloning feature, choose the "Copy" and "Paste" commands to create a copy of the objects.

To flip the clones, use your software's "Flip horizontal" command or flip tool. If neither feature is available, group the two objects and drag the left transformation handle all the way across, past the right side of the image. Simultaneously pressing shift will ensure a symmetric reflection.

After flipping the two objects, drag the vertical line so that it aligns exactly with the vertical line in the cross. Both windows now occupy the same relative positions, with reference to the center line.

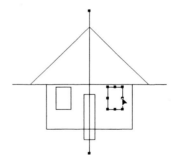

Select the window shape and vertical line, clone them, flip them, and move them into position, as shown above.

The basic form of the house is now complete. We no longer need the horizontal and vertical lines of the cross, so select all three perpendicular lines and delete them from your drawing. Next, select both the large rectangle that represents the body of the house and the triangle that represents the roof. Fill these two shapes with solid black. Now select the window and doorway shapes and fill them with solid white. None of the shapes should be stroked.

After filling the shapes in your house drawing, choose the "Preview" command, or the equivalent. The house should look something like this.

The next step is to draw a long horizontal line along the bottom of the house to represent the ground level. Use the line tool, polygon tool, or Bézier curve tool to draw a long horizontal line flush with the bottom of the house.

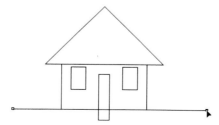

Create the ground-level line by drawing a horizontal line aligned with the bottom of the large rectangle.

The next image we will create is the tree. As you may recall from the picture of the finished ornament, the tree is even more simplified than the house, being no more than a fat line with a circle on top. We will create the circle first.

Select the ellipse tool. Starting about even with the top of the roof and an inch or so to its left, press the shift key and drag down and to the right to draw a circle as shown in the figure below.

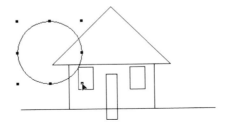

Create the top of the tree by drawing a perfect circle with the ellipse tool. If your ellipse tool draws from center to corner or from arc to arc, you may have to reposition the shape with the arrow tool.

To create the trunk of the tree, draw a vertical line with the line tool, polygon tool, or Bézier curve tool.

In the picture of the finished ornament, the paths representing the ground and the tree are either heavy lines or shapes with heavy outlines. These paths therefore need to be stroked. Select the ground path and stroke it with a black, 2-point line weight. Select the circle, fill it with solid white, and stroke it with a black, 2-point line weight. Select the tree trunk and stroke it with a black, 4-point line weight.

After filling and stroking the tree and ground paths, the house ornament will preview as shown above.

Unlike the picture of the finished ornament, our tree appears in front of our house. In addition, the ground path overlaps the doorway. Because we created these paths after the paths that make up the house, they appear in front of the house. Select the ground path, the circle, and the tree trunk and choose a "Send to back" command, or the equivalent.

Send the most recent paths behind the older paths that make up the house. The ornament now bears closer resemblance to the picture at the beginning of the chapter.

To create the fence, we won't draw a single line. Instead, we'll simply duplicate and reshape lines that already exist. Not only will this save us the trouble of drawing new paths and applying additional strokes and fills, but the duplication will also lend consistency to the image as a whole.

In the picture of the finished ornament, you may have noticed that the tree trunk is the same height and line weight as each of the three fence posts. Therefore, clone the tree trunk path and drag it directly horizontally to a spot about ⅛ inch to the right of the house. Create another clone and move it about ¼ inch farther to the right. If your software offers a "Duplicate" or "Transform again" command, choose it to create a third clone, nudged to the right another ¼ inch. If not, clone the line a third time and move it manually.

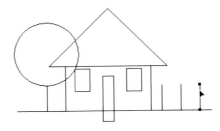

Create the fence posts by cloning the tree trunk three times and repositioning the clones at regular intervals.

To create the horizontal slats in the fence, we will use duplicates of the ground path. Select this path and clone it. Drag the clone directly upward so it sits on top of the three fence posts. The line is now in the proper position; but unfortunately, it is far too long, extending through the house and into the tree. To make the line shorter, select it with your program's arrow tool or reshape tool and drag the left end of the line to the right until it rests just inside the house, as shown below.

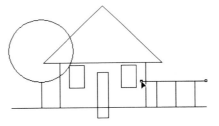

Move the left-hand point of the cloned line to the right side of the house. This slightly shorter version of the ground path serves as the topmost slat in the fence.

Clone the slat and drag the clone about ⅛ inch directly downward to create a second slat.

To make the slats stand out a little from the rest of the fence, we will add a line effect. Select both slats and stroke them with a 4-point line weight. Then clone the selected paths, position the clones exactly in front of the originals, and apply a white stroke with a 2-point line weight to each clone. A white line will now appear to be drawn through the middle of each slat, creating the "in-line" effect described in Chapter 4. This simple line effect gives the the slats a hint of depth, setting the fence apart slightly from the rest of the ornament.

The only remaining step is to clean up the illustration. For example, you may need to reposition a few objects. Or maybe you need to reshape the roof because it doesn't appear entirely symmetrical. Perhaps some of the lines in the fence aren't quite flush with each other. In short, your drawing may have several problems, or none at all. This is the time to examine your drawing and make corrections.

Our drawing has only one problem: the slats in the fence appear in front of the house, but they should be in back. Select all seven paths that make up the fence (the two white slat lines, the two black slat lines, and the three posts) by marqueeing them with the arrow tool. Then choose the "Send to back" command or the equivalent to place the fence behind the house.

The completed ornament, with fence sent to back, appears as shown above.

Your page ornament is now finished. If you have not already done so, you should save your drawing to disk for future use or for importing into a page-layout or presentation application. If you would like to see your drawing on paper, print the file.

———— ◆ ▪●▪ ◆ ————

This ends our first basic sample project. We have demonstrated how to create a typical page ornament using the line, rectangle, and ellipse tools. We have also demonstrated how to layer objects, how to duplicate objects, and how to apply a simple line effect.

When creating page ornaments of your own, remember to keep your drawings as simple as possible. They should also be easily recognizable, yet generic enough to be used over and over again. Finally, try to sketch the basic form of your central shape and then work outward. This will save you time and will help you to avoid the frustration of having to redraw fundamental graphic elements.

In our next project, we will use more basic tools and techniques to create a simple cartoon.

Creating a simple cartoon

Our second project in this chapter is to create a simple cartoon. Cartoons can be used to brighten up an otherwise dull page in an informal document or to draw attention to a humorous article. We will be creating a cartoon of a bland-looking character unenthusiastically raising his fingers in a V-for-victory gesture with the caption "We're Number Two." Such a cartoon might be used to rally the troops, indicating that anything less than first place is unthinkable.

We're
Number
Two.

Our second sample project is to create this deadpan cartoon character.

In many ways, a cartoon is the opposite of a page ornament, the subject of our previous sample project. Rather than being generally appropriate for a wide variety of documents, a cartoon has a more specific purpose, making it appropriate for some projects and inappropriate for others.

Cartoons are perfect for at least three kinds of publications:

1. Informal publications. For example, you might want to include at least one cartoon in every edition of a newsletter. It makes the publication seem both friendly and sympathetic, rather than something you should read for your own good.

2. Trade publications. If your publication is the kind that gets distributed to a large group of people, but rarely gets read, a cartoon may be the answer. Cartoons get read more often and more regularly than any other portion of a publication.

3. "Cutting-edge" publications. A successful cartoon is a hip slice of social documentary, which demonstrates that your publication has a specific awareness for audience entertainment as well as for education.

By contrast, cartoons should *not* appear in formal or legal documents, such as business letters or contracts. Nor are they suited to serious publications, such as reports and statements, that are to be read by only a select group of people. Cartoons are populist graphics for popular publications.

Another way in which cartoons differ from page ornaments is that they may only be used once. Very few cartoons are funny or interesting to read a second time. A recycled cartoon can make a publication seem cheap rather than innovative.

Above are some more examples of cartoons. Each graphic is fanciful rather than realistic, and therefore well suited to an informal publication. You can see how they might add flair to an accompanying article. The best of cartoons inspire interest immediately.

At first glance, the sample cartoon we will be creating may appear intimidating rather than simple. But as you will see, there is very little to draw in this graphic. Many features are repeated over and over again, so the degree of difficulty and the amount of time required to complete this project is less than you might expect.

The first portion that we will draw is our character's head. The shape we create for the head is very important, since we will be copying and transforming it later to create the character's nose, fingers, and thumb.

Select the freehand tool. Because this tool is so easy to operate, we will be relying on it as the primary drawing tool throughout this graphic. If you are new to drawing with this tool, you may want to raise the freehand tool *tolerance level*, thus instructing your software to smooth out your lines during the calculation process. The tolerance level generally ranges from 1 to 10, with 1 resulting in tight paths that follow your exact movements as you draw with the freehand tool and 10 resulting in very loose paths that ignore almost all sharp corners and other possible inaccuracies. In most programs, the freehand tolerance option may be accessed by choosing a "Preferences" command or double-clicking the freehand tool icon. Not all drawing programs offer a freehand tolerance option.

After you have selected the freehand tool and specified a tolerance level, draw the pickle-shaped outline shown in the figure below.

Draw the basic form of our character's head using the freehand tool. If your first attempt doesn't even remotely resemble our path, delete the shape and try again.

Don't expect to get this path right the first time, or even the second or third. Several attempts were required to achieve the pickle line shown in our figure. Once you do get a line that appears vaguely accurate, use your software's arrow tool or reshape feature to relocate points and adjust Bézier control handles as discussed in the *Reshaping paths* section of Chapter 3.

Congratulations, you have just completed one of the most difficult steps in creating this image! Incidentally, don't waste too much time making your path look exactly like ours. As we mentioned earlier, it is preferable that you try to demonstrate your personal style throughout these sample projects by deviating slightly from our figures in whatever manner you see fit.

The next portion of the cartoon person we will create is his nose. We will base the nose on the shape of the head. As in the previous project, the first step in creating one form based on another is to duplicate the existing form. Using the arrow tool, select the line we just drew. Then clone (or copy and paste) the free-form path and drag it to the right an inch or so.

The next step in creating the cartoon nose is to flip the selected clone vertically. Choose the "Flip vertical" command or use your program's flip tool. If neither feature is available, shift-drag the top transformation handle all the way down past the bottom of the image.

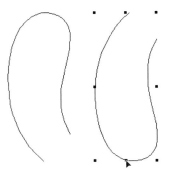

Flipping the clone vertically produces a reflection of the original path.

Though some of us come pretty close, no one's nose is as large as his or her head. Therefore, the cartoon nose must be reduced. In most applications, you may reduce this path by dragging at the one of the transformation handles. To ensure a proportional reduction, drag at a corner handle and press the shift key if necessary. In other applications, you may have to use a special scaling tool.

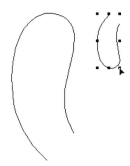

Drag one of the four corner transformations handles toward the image to reduce the nose to a more reasonable size.

While the nose is still selected, choose the "Copy" command to transfer a copy of the selected element to the clipboard in your computer's memory. We will retrieve the copy later when we create the hand.

This is almost all there is to creating the nose. The selected line may not look much like a nose, but once we get it into position, you'll be surprised how well it works. But before we drag the nose into place, we will create our character's eyeglasses. Because one lens is behind the nose and the other is in front, it is easier to put the glasses and nose together before moving them inside the face.

We will first create the bar of the glasses that goes over the bridge of the nose. Select the freehand tool and draw a slightly curved line joining both ends of the nose at the top, closing the shape off so that its interior is completely enclosed. If your software does not allow you to extend an existing path by drawing on it with the freehand tool, create the slightly curved line as a separate path and group the two shapes.

Next, we draw the glasses. To create the first lens, select the ellipse tool and draw a relatively tall, thin oval, about the same size and proportions of the nose.

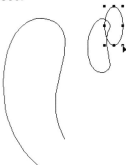

Draw the first eye with the ellipse tool. You may either draw it at the location shown above, or create the shape and then move it into position.

Since one lens is the same size and shape as the other, we can clone the existing oval to create the second lens. Select the ellipse with the arrow tool, clone it, and move the clone so it rests on the left side of the nose as shown in the figure below.

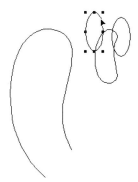

The clone of the first eye acts as the second. Here, the place-ment of the clone is very important, since it must appear to rest on the nose.

Applying Your Knowledge

Select the three face elements—the two ellipses and the nose shape—and drag them into the upper portion of the head so our man appears to be looking left, as shown in the following figure.

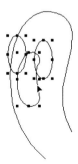

Drag the nose and eyes into position inside the head path.

While the three face elements remain selected, stroke the three paths with black, 2-point line weights and apply solid white fills. Then select the large head path and stroke it with a black, 3-point line weight. The head path should not be filled.

After stroking and filling the shapes in your face, choose the "Preview" command, or the equivalent. The face should look something like this.

If you preview your face thus far, you will notice a couple problems with the image. First of all, the left lens image overlaps the nose, but it should appear behind the nose. If we send it to back, it will appear behind the head path, which is also incorrect. To correct the problem, you may either select both the left lens and head path and send them to back, or select both the nose and right lens and bring them to front.

The second problem is a bit more complicated. Notice that a segment connects the right side of the nose with the right lens, as if the nose is somehow separated from the face. The face will appear more natural if this segment is deleted. Different programs allow you to delete segments in different ways. In some programs, you select the shape with a reshape tool, select the points above and below the segment you want to delete, and choose a special "Break" or "Split" command. In other programs, you click above and below the segment with a scissors tool or a knife tool.

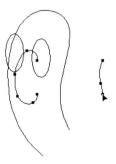

In this figure, we have removed a segment from the right side of the nose path. Both the nose and the removed segment (right) are displayed in the reshape mode so we can view all points in both paths. The points in your paths may vary; however, the removed segment should be about the same size as the one shown above.

After you remove the segment, delete it from your drawing. So that the nose path doesn't appear to end too abruptly, stroke it with a round cap.

If your software doesn't allow you to delete segments or split paths, never fear; a work-around exists. Select the rectangle tool and draw a rectangle that covers the segment you would otherwise delete. It may also cover some of the right lens, but it should not overlap the left side of the nose or any of the head path. Fill the rectangle with solid white and apply no stroke. Finally, select the right lens shape with the arrow tool and layer it in front of the other objects in the drawing.

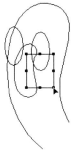

If you use a low-end drawing program, cover the right side of the nose with a white rectangle. Then bring the right ellipse to the front of the drawing.

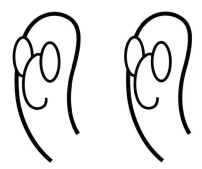

When you preview your drawing, the face will look like the one on the left if you delete a segment and apply a stroke with a round cap. If you use a white rectangle to hide the right side of the nose, the end of the line will appear flat, as shown in the image on the right.

The only feature still missing from the face is the mouth. Select the freehand tool and draw a very small, frowning mouth starting at the left side of the face as shown below. Stroke the mouth with a black, 2-point line weight and round caps and apply no fill.

A small, downturned mouth on our character makes him appear sympathetic, but not morosely unhappy.

To create hair, we could draw a bunch of little lines on the top of our character's head using the freehand tool or the line tool. However, not only would this be time-consuming, it would also increase the size of your drawing on disk without enhancing the appearance of the cartoon noticeably. An easier way to give our man a hair is to draw a great pompadour with the freehand tool.

Draw a wavy leaf shape with the freehand tool to create our man's bouffant hairdo. The path should be closed, so be sure to drag all the way back to the first point in the shape. As

was probably the case when drawing the head path, you may have to make several attempts to draw the shape satisfactorily. You may also reshape the path after drawing it.

Fill the hair shape with a light gray tint (around 20% to 30% black) and stroke the shape with a black, 1-point outline.

Our cartoon man is still missing ears. Luckily, these cartoon ears won't require much detail, since your viewer won't pay much attention to them. Any blob on the side of a head is assumed by most viewers to be an ear. First, draw a circle with the ellipse tool just below the hair on the right side of the head. Fill the circle with solid white and apply no stroke.

The first step in creating the ear is to draw a simple circle.

Next, clone the circle and layer it directly in front of the original. Ungroup this shape or convert it to curves. Then remove a small segment from the left portion of the circle to make it appear that it's attached to the head. (Use the same method described earlier for removing a segment from the nose.) Stroke this path with a black, 2-point line weight with round caps and apply no fill.

If your software does not allow you to ungroup geometric shapes, do not clone the circle, but simply stroke the original circle with a black, 2-point line weight. Then draw a small white rectangle to cover the left side of the circle.

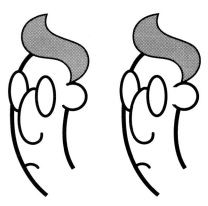

When you preview your drawing, the ear will look like the one on the left if you delete a segment and apply a stroke with a round cap. If you use a white rectangle to hide the left side of the ear, the ends of the circle will appear flat, as shown in the image on the right.

To create the inside of the ear, draw a small circle inside the circle representing the ear. Stroke this circle with a black, 2-point line weight. Then clone this circle and offset it a single point to the right of the original. Fill the clone with solid white and apply no stroke.

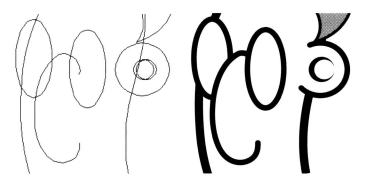

In the enlarged view on the left, we see the two circles that make up the inside of the ear. The rear circle is stroked, the forward circle is filled with white. The enlarged preview on the right displays the result.

Applying Your Knowledge

The next few steps involve more drawing with the freehand tool. To create our man's collar, draw a triangular path on each side of his neck as shown in the following figure.

Draw the two triangles of the collar using the freehand tool. Notice that both triangles overlap the bottom of the head path. Also, don't worry about getting the two triangles to meet exactly with each other. As you can see above, the left triangle rides higher than the right one, creating a cock-eyed effect that is appropriate in a cartoon.

Select both collar triangles with the arrow tool and apply black, 2-point strokes and white fills.

The tie is easy to create. Using the ellipse tool, draw the knot of the tie just below the base of the neck, so that it fits snugly into the collar. Then send the circle to back so that it appears behind the collar.

Draw the main portion of the tie with the freehand tool with the same flourish and recklessness we used to draw the hair. Feel free to make it big and fat; this guy's no fashion expert.

Draw the tie in a quick, general motion. Close the path by dragging all the way back to the first point in the shape. You may of course reshape the path after you draw it.

Fill both tie shapes with the same light black tint used to fill the hair. Also stroke the shape with a black, 1-point outline.

Just for fun, we might as well give our man a tie clasp. It will be easy to do, and it'll make him look even more inept. We will base the tie clasp on the shape we used for the inside of the ear. Select both the stroked and white-filled circles inside the ear and clone them. Drag these clones down to the middle of the fattest portion of the tie. Then group the circles and rotate them 90° using your software's "Rotate" command or rotation tool.

Clone the circles that make up the inside of the ear, move them inside the tie, and rotate them 90° to form the clasp.

Applying Your Knowledge

The next step is the lengthiest and most demanding drawing step. Using the freehand tool, we will draw the entire body of our cartoon character, including arms and paunch. Draw the lines as shown below. If you make a big mistake, delete the path and try again. If you make a small mistake, reshape the path or just delete a couple points and redraw them.

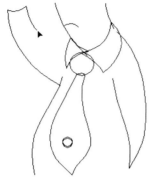

Using the freehand tool, draw the right arm and the right side of the body as a single V-shape. This makes the arm appear behind the back, allowing us to avoid drawing the right hand. The paunch is one arcing line. The left arm is the most difficult feature, since it is fully visible and gesturing upward. To create this path, we draw three consecutive curves.

Select the three body paths and send them to the back of the drawing, so they are covered by the collar. Then stroke the paths with a black, 3-point line weight. Use round caps if available. Apply no fill.

The only part of the cartoon character left to be created is his hand. Many beginning artists are intimidated by hands. The fingers are hard to draw correctly in relation to each other—especially the thumb—and it is often difficult to fit all the fingers on the same hand. Also, hands are capable of complex movements that can be difficult to render.

Our hand is different. First of all, very little drawing is required. Each of the fingers, including the thumb, will be created from an existing graphic element.

Remember when we copied the nose earlier in the drawing? Well, now we're ready to use it. Choose the "Paste" command and the nose will appear on your page as it looked before we added the bridge of the glasses and deleted the segment that separated the nose from the face. If necessary, drag the selected path away from the cartoon onto a blank area of your page. Then flip it vertically. This completes our first element, the index finger. Incidentally, you may have noticed that by flipping the copy of the nose we have come full circle—the index finger is merely a reduced replica of the head.

Next, clone the path. This will be the second finger raised in the victory sign.

Then choose the "Paste" command again and rotate the selected path 270° (or –90°). The resulting element will be the thumb.

Choose "Paste" a third time and reduce the newest path slightly, to about 80% of its original size. Then clone the path. These two elements will be the other fingers in the hand.

Shown to the left of the face are the five transformed copies of the nose that will make up the hand, including the flipped first and second fingers, the rotated thumb, and the reduced third and fourth fingers.

We now have all the raw materials with which to build our hand. Drag the index finger to a location about a half inch above and slightly to the left of the left arm. Move the second finger next to the index finger, and rotate it about 20° so that it stands out from the index finger slightly. Move the third and fourth fingers so they are to the left of the second finger and extend halfway below it. Then move the thumb to a location between the index finger and the arm.

Drag each of the fingers into position as shown above.

The fingers are all in their correct locations, but they aren't quite a hand. Some additional transformations are required. To begin with, we must establish the correct layering order. The forth finger should be behind the third, which is behind the second, which is behind the first, which is behind the thumb. Probably the easiest way to accomplish this is to select the four finger paths and choose the "Send to back" command (or equivalent). The deselect the index finger, choose "Send to back" again, and so on, until only the last one (the fourth finger) is selected and sent to back.

Now that we have placed all the fingers in their correct locations, we see that the following size adjustments are also required: Reduce the third finger vertically to 90% to add a bit of perspective to the hand. Likewise, reduce the fourth finger vertically to 80%. Then reduce the thumb horizontally to 80% so that it more accurately fits the shape of the hand.

Finally, we must add a single line to bring the fingers together. Start drawing with the freehand tool at the bottom right point in the index finger. Your path should extend across the back of the hand and around the palm as shown in the following figure.

Extend the path of the index finger to include the back of the hand and the palm.

If you cannot extend a path with the freehand tool, draw the back of the hand and the palm as a separate object, and send the finished path to back. Select all paths in the hand and apply a black, 2-point stroke and a white fill.

If you have not missed any steps, your hand will print as shown on the facing page.

The five paths combine to form a single hand when the cartoon is previewed or printed.

We have only two steps left. The first is to create the text. But before you enter the text from the keyboard, you may want to establish the type specifications. Change the font to Times and the type style to plain; change the alignment to centered; and change the type size to 24-point. Then select the text tool and click well below the cartoon figure, horizontally even with the bottom tip of his tie. In some programs, a special dialog box will appear that provides a text-entry area.

Since we want each word to be on a separate line, you must enter a paragraph return between each word. Thus, enter the text , "We're¶Number¶Two." The symbol ¶ means to press the return key. If your program provides a dialog box for entering text, click the OK button to display the text on your page.

The final step is the same as the final step in the previous sample project: clean-up. The number of corrections and enhancements required to complete a graphic increases with its complexity. This cartoon is a case in point. Our page ornament required very little clean-up; our more complex cartoon requires quite a bit. Of course, the exact amount will depend on your personal preference.

We're
Number
Two.

This is our completed cartoon, after adding text and adding a few details with the freehand tool.

Typically, clean-up is accomplished using the freehand and Bézier curve tools in a magnified view size. To refine the previous figure, we have added a button and a cuff to the left sleeve; we have added folds to both the right and left sleeves; we have added shadows behind the hair and the tie; and we added highlights to the hair. All these additions—except the cuff line—were made by creating small paths that we filled with either solid black or solid white without applying any stroke. The cuff line received no fill and a black, 2-point stroke. These are the kinds of changes you can make to your graphic as well.

After you have executed whatever clean-up work you deem necessary, you should save your drawing to disk if you have not already done so. And as before, you may print your cartoon or combine the graphic with text and other drawings in a page-layout or presentation application.

This ends the second of two sample projects included in this chapter. This project demonstrated how to use the freehand tool, how to reshape and transform images, how to use a single path over and over in other situations, and how to think your way through an informal illustration.

The next two chapters contain more sample projects, with increasing levels of difficulty. If you feel that you have successfully completed this project and understand the techniques, tools, and commands covered, you will probably have little difficulty moving on to the intermediate-level projects. If you feel unsure of any point that we covered, or are not satisfied with your work, you may want to re-examine earlier chapters, or perhaps try out some basic sample projects of your own.

Intermediate Hands-On Projects

CHAPTER 6

This chapter is the second of three chapters that provide step-by-step explanations of the creation of specific graphics using a drawing application. We discuss each of the features and methods introduced in Chapters 1 through 4 while working toward an actual goal. All projects are "hands-on," demonstrating how to create free-form computer artwork according to easy-to-follow, concise guidelines.

In this chapter, we will create two intermediate-level graphics: the silhouette of a human form and a company logo. Each project concentrates on fairly difficult aspects of graphic composition. If you have not yet completed the graphics in the previous chapter, we advise you to at least read through them at this time. By becoming familiar with the techniques, tools, and commands covered in Chapter 5, you will be more prepared to create the graphics in this chapter.

As the difficulty of our projects increases, it is increasingly important that you don't get hung up trying to match your graphics to ours dot-for-dot. As we mentioned in the last chapter, it is preferable that you try to work your own style into each project. By following our directions in a manner that seems comfortable to you, you may learn personal drawing habits that will be helpful when you create artwork in the future.

Creating a human silhouette

Our first intermediate project is to create the silhouette of a human form. Silhouettes can be very useful illustrations, since they are both realistic and relatively easy to create. Also, drawing a silhouette provides an opportunity for you to concentrate on the overall form of an object, without being overwhelmed by details that may not only slow down the creation of a graphic, but may even detract from its appearance.

Our third sample project is a silhouette of a young girl.

Because silhouettes do not display facial features, they tend to be more generic, more useful in situations that display a typical person performing a typical task. By the same token, however, they do not elicit a viewer's empathy. For example, suppose your company shares one or two photo copiers that seem to be breaking down continually. A silhouette drawing of a copier repair-person would be the perfect accompaniment for an article on this subject in a company newsletter or memorandum. After all, repair-persons are probably a common sight in your building, but they are not in the company's direct employ and the article is undoubtedly not intended for their eyes. A silhouette basically tells the reader: you are not this person, but you know the function that this person serves in the company, and he or she is somehow involved in this article.

Silhouettes also typically serve well as embellishments for "serious" publications, such as reports, directories, manuals, and so on, which require realistic graphics rather than cartoons or highly stylized drawings. Since you can make silhouettes appear realistic without rendering large amounts of time and effort in their creation, they are the perfect last-minute graphic for a serious publication.

Above are more examples of silhouette drawings. Each graphic is both realistic and generic, ideal for decorating a neutral, no-nonsense publication.

As always, we will begin our drawing by creating a central sketch and working outward. However, this time, we will create the sketch in a painting software, such as MacPaint. Later, we will import the finished sketch into a drawing program to be traced by hand, or with the software's trace tool.

Sketching the silhouette

As we discussed in Chapter 1, a painting application is the ideal environment for sketching ideas, since it offers tools that closely resemble artist's traditional tools. For example, when you sketch with pencil on paper, you draw a few lines with the pencil, erase a few stray marks with an eraser, sketch some more with the pencil, and so on, alternating between drawing and undrawing to refine your artwork. A painting program offers pencil and eraser tools that are used in the same manner as they are in real life. Drawing programs offer no such equivalents.

If you use a drawing program, such as Canvas or SuperPaint, that provides both drawing and painting tools, you may create your sketch and trace it in the same application.

To begin this project, start up your painting program. Any paint program will do. If you don't own any painting software, we heartily suggest that you purchase one, since painting software is both useful and inexpensive. Short of that, you may skip the sketching portion of this project to the *Tracing the silhouette* section later in this chapter. At this point, substitute a piece of bitmapped clip-art in place of the sketch. Many drawing programs include bitmapped art to demonstrate their tracing capabilities. If you own neither a painting program nor any bitmapped artwork, at least read along with our text although you won't be participating.

Sometimes the easiest way to create a naturalistic form is to start with a geometric sketch that you have created using one or more of your painting program's shape tools. These tools operate identically or very similarly to the shape tools in your drawing program. After the rigid structure is finished, it can then be softened using the pencil or paintbrush tool.

We will begin our geometric sketch by creating the head. Select the oval tool and draw an oval as shown below.

Draw an oval to represent the basic form of the head.

This oval will act as the basic form of the skull of the silhouette's head. To this skull, we will add the general outline of the facial features using the polygon shape tool. In a painting program, the polygon tool is operated as it is in a drawing program: You click at various points on your screen to create a connected series of straight lines as you go, one line between each click point. The polygon tool stops creating lines when you double-click or close the shape. Select the polygon tool and draw the profile shown below.

Using the polygon tool, we sketch the nose and jaw line of the girl's face. Each corner in the outline of the face is a point where we clicked with the cursor.

A bow is tied in the girl's hair, pulling it into a bun that curls evenly into the back of her head. To sketch the bun, we again use the oval tool. Select the oval tool and draw a vertically oriented ellipse.

This second ellipse represents the bun of hair at the back of the girl's head.

The last feature of the head that we will sketch is the bow. We select the polygon tool for this task, and draw the shape shown below.

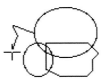

Sketching the bow with the polygon tool completes the silhouette's head.

Notice that throughout this quick sketch of the head with the oval and polygon tools, we have made no attempt to draw eyes, or a mouth, or any other incidental facial feature. In sketching, we are concerned only with the general outline of the human form, not any of its details.

The next step is to sketch the body. This is a little more difficult than the sketching we have done so far, since the body is made up of irregular shapes and protrusions. However, using the polygon tool, it is an easier task than it might otherwise have been.

Draw the irregular outline of the body using the polygon tool. If you make a mistake, double-click to end the outline, choose the "Undo" command to erase it, and then try again.

Now that the basic form of the major portion of the body is completed, we have to sketch only the legs. In fact, we have only one leg to sketch, since the left leg is hidden entirely behind the right. In a normal illustration, it would be difficult to hide one limb entirely behind another like this and get away with it. But in a silhouette, we have more freedom to pick and choose what we want to draw and what we want to leave to the viewer's imagination.

Sketch the right leg with the polygon tool as shown above. We don't need to worry about the left leg, since it is presumably so very slightly visible that it does not affect the basic form of the silhouette.

Our basic sketch is complete. You have probably noticed that some refinement will be required to make the sketch look less angular and more naturalistic. This is where your painting program's unique tools can be used to great advantage. We will fill the silhouette sketch with solid black using the fill tool. This tool most commonly looks like a tipped can of paint. Because the fill tool fills a shape from border to border, we must erase those portions of each outline that combine to form smaller shapes within our larger silhouette. To prepare for using the fill tool, we will first erase these overlapping outlines. As shown in the following figure, only one swipe of the eraser tool is required to destroy all barriers inside the silhouette.

Applying Your Knowledge

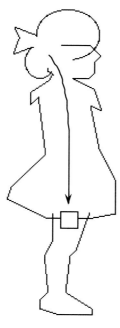

Using the eraser tool, carve away any barriers that act as borders for smaller shapes inside the sketch and would therefore prevent the paint from flowing throughout. The arrow indicates the movement of our cursor.

Now select the fill tool and make sure that the selected fill pattern is solid black. Then click anywhere inside the sketch. If your entire screen suddenly becomes black, there is a break somewhere in the outline of your sketch. Choose the "Undo" command and then try to locate the break. You may have to look carefully, since a break may be only one pixel wide. Once you locate the break, fix it using the pencil tool or the paintbrush tool in "fat-bits," and try filling the sketch again.

Fill the sketch with solid black using the fill tool.

Before we soften the harsh corners of our sketch, we must fill in one remaining detail—the bow on the back of the girl's dress. We skipped this feature earlier because it is more fluid than other portions of the silhouette and cannot be expressed easily as a geometric sketch. Instead, we will draw this form using the filled freehand shape tool, typically displayed in your paint program toolbox as an icon filled with gray. The filled freehand tool will enable us to create the shape and fill it in the same motion.

You draw with the freehand tool in the same way you operate the freehand tool in a drawing program—simply drag your cursor about the screen. If you are unhappy with the shape that you create, choose the "Undo" command and try again.

Applying Your Knowledge

The first example shows us using the filled freehand tool to draw the bow at the back of the girl's dress. The second example displays the finished bow.

The next step can be fairly time-consuming, since you will have to perform it largely without our direction. We will soften the harsh angularity of our sketch using the pencil or paintbrush tool in a magnified view size. Many portions of our sketch are too severe, too geometric. Zoom in to an area that has a sharp corner. Then select the pencil tool and click on some black dots to erase them, rounding off the corner. If your pencil tool does not erase black pixels, select white as your color and use the pencil or paintbrush tool. You may also add dots as you see fit.

After you have completed one corner, return to the normal view size, locate another sharp corner, and repeat the process. Eventually, you should wind up with an image similar to the more naturalistic silhouette shown in the following figure.

Notice how the silhouette appears softened now that we have rounded off the geometric corners using the pencil tool in "fat-bits." We also added a small detail—the ribbon end of the bow in her hair.

Our little girl is much softer, more fluid in appearance, and therefore more realistic. As a matter of fact, if we wanted to, we could stop sketching right now. Technically, this sketch is polished enough to be used in a wide variety of situations. The only problem is its flatness; it looks more like a cardboard cutout than a real human being. To remedy this, we will add some white details that, while not absolutely necessary, develop the drawing in a more interesting direction.

Suppose that our girl has white socks. This will help to highlight the form of her legs and add a spark of detail by displaying the outline of the shoes.

Select the pencil or paintbrush tool and draw the boundaries of the shoe and sock as three white lines against the black silhouette.

Drawing with the pencil tool against a black background creates a white line. This allows us to carve the outline of the shoe and sock.

If you have problems drawing smooth lines with the pencil or paintbrush tool in a normal view size, zoom in and then try to draw. It is often easier to draw with the pencil tool or the paintbrush tool in a magnified view size.

Make sure that your lines extend off into the white area of the page, so that the three black areas of the shoe and sock are entirely isolated from each other and from the rest of the silhouette. The reason for this is that we need to fill two of these black areas with white paint using the fill tool.

After you have completed the shoe and sock outlines, select the fill tool and the solid white pattern. Click with the fill tool inside the main sock area, making it white. If the white leaks into other areas of the silhouette, such as the upper body or the shoe, you did not properly isolate these areas when creating the white lines with the pencil or paintbrush. In such a case, choose the "Undo" command to return the silhouette to black, locate the dot or dots that are connecting the black areas, and erase them using the pencil tool in "fat-bits." Then try to fill the sock again.

The other area that we need to fill with white is the portion of the sock showing through the top of the shoe. Click in this area with the fill tool as well. Once again, if an additional black area becomes white, the area was not properly isolated, and you must try again as we described in the previous paragraph.

Fill the two areas of the sock with white using the fill tool.

Our final step is to create one more white detail, similar to the sock. This time, we will add a white glove hanging at the girl's side, the finishing touch to her formal Sunday attire. Using the pencil or

Applying Your Knowledge

paintbrush tool, draw a white outline of the general form of a hand, as shown in the figure below. As you can see, the hand is not particularly detailed, so you probably won't find it too difficult to draw.

After you close the outline, select the fill tool and solid white pattern, and click inside the glove to fill it with white.

Draw the outline of the girl's glove as a closed outline, as shown on the left. Then fill the enclosed area with white using the fill tool.

This completes our sketch of the silhouette of a young girl. If you like, you can add a few more small details. For example, in the figure above, we have added a shine to the toe of the shoe.

If you have not already done so, you should save the sketch to disk. If you want to see your drawing on paper, print the file. Then quit your painting program and start your drawing program, in which we will be tracing the sketch.

Tracing the silhouette

After you start your drawing program, create a new file and import your bitmapped sketch (or clip-art, if you skipped the sketching procedure). In some programs, you are invited to open a tracing template when you create a new file. In others, you import the sketch using an "Import" command. Still other programs can open paint files directly, provided they are saved in either the MacPaint or TIFF format.

After you import the sketch into your drawing program, it will display in the drawing window. In some programs, the sketch will appear grayed, as shown above, to distinguish it from the points and paths of your drawing.

We will be tracing this image using your software's trace tool. If your program does not offer a trace tool, you'll have to trace the image on your own, using the freehand tool.

Before tracing the sketch, you may want to adjust the sensitivity of the trace tool. In most programs, you access sensitivity options by choosing a "Preferences" command or by double-clicking the trace tool. If your software allows you to select between tracing an image with a polygon or with Bézier curve, select the Bézier curve option. Otherwise, your software should use Bézier curves automatically.

Your software may offer any number of options for adjusting the sensitivity of the trace tool. For specific information, consult the documentation that came with your application. However, most programs offer some sort of tracking option. Typically, the tracking may vary between 1 and 10, with 1 resulting in tight paths that follow the exact shape of the sketch and 10 resulting in loose paths that ignore sharp corners and other possible inconsistencies. If your sketch is very accurate, use a lower value. If you feel that your sketch is rough or sloppy, use a higher value. In some programs, the freehand tolerance option (discussed in Chapter 5) also affects the performance of the trace tool.

After you have selected the trace tool and specified a sensitivity level, trace the sketched image as described in the *Operating the trace tool* section of Chapter 3. This may involve clicking next to the sketch or marqueeing the entire image. If you operate your trace tool by clicking, you will have to click at least three times—once to trace the black area of the girl's head and body, a second time to trace the white glove, and a third time to trace the shoe. You may also have to specify the fill for each path. The main silhouette and shoe shapes should be filled with solid black. The glove should be filled with white.

After tracing and filling the shapes in the silhouette, we preview the image. Because our sketch contained no stray pixels, the traced paths are surprisingly accurate. However, all paths will require some reshaping.

The accuracy of your traced image will vary depending on the accuracy of your sketch, the sensitivity setting for your trace tool, and the sophistication of your software. Your trace may look better or worse than the one shown in the preceding figure. But regardless of how well your trace tool performs, some reshaping will be required. Points will have to be moved, added, and subtracted. Bézier control handles will need to be adjusted.

In the preceding figure, for example, the bow in the girl's hair appears slightly lopsided. The ribbon below the bow ends in pinched little gnarls rather than an elegant *V*. This area will benefit from being reshaped.

Applying Your Knowledge

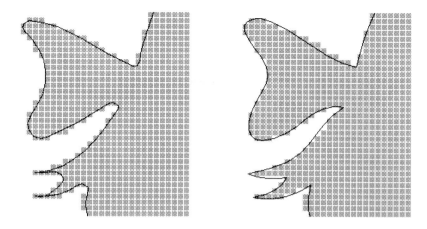

Shown on the left is an enlarged view of the path created by the trace tool. The path traces the grayed pixels of the hair bow. The traced path is more or less accurate, but it lacks character. Curves are too flat, corners are rounded off, and segments between points are too straight. To fix these problems, we reshape the path as shown on the right. The curves now appear more natural and segments meet to form crisp corners.

You may think that our example seems like nit-picking. However, you'll find that most tracing inaccuracies turn out to be problems of minor detail. Though unimportant on their own, these details combine to improve or impair your illustration.

Since your traced paths will look slightly different than ours, we cannot guide you step by step through the reshaping process. But we can offer a few words of advice. First, every corner in your sketch should receive a corner point. Only a few places—like the head, the top of the collar, and the front of the skirt—will require smooth points. Also, like most naturalistic images, this drawing should contain no straight segment. All segments should curve to some extent, which means that every point must offer two Bézier control handles. (If your software does not offer Bézier control handles, your entire freehand path should be smoothed.)

The final bit of advice is the most important: be patient. This is your chance to become familiar with your software's reshaping capabilities. Your experimentation will lead to a mastery of the drawing environment and an increased understanding of your program's tools and commands.

This image is the result of 30 minutes of reshaping and redrawing traced paths. Notice that both bows flow more smoothly, and details like the nose and knee appear more distinct. The shoe and glove show the most obvious change. Because the shoe was so badly executed by the trace tool, this path was redrawn from scratch.

After you have finished the reshaping and redrawing your paths, you should save your drawing to disk. You may also print your silhouette or combine it with text and other images in a page-layout or presentation application.

This ends our third sample project. We have demonstrated how to create a naturalistic sketch in a painting program, how to use common paint program tools, how to import a sketch into a drawing program for use as a tracing template, and how to use the trace tool to convert a jagged bitmapped image into a smooth illustration.

Silhouettes grab reader attention without demanding reader empathy. Since silhouettes are realistic graphics and require little effort to create, they are ideally suited to serious publications with tight production schedules.

When drawing a silhouette, try sketching the form in a painting application using geometric shape tools like the oval tool and the polygon tool. Then fill the sketch with black and soften the harsh edges with the pencil or paintbrush tool. To enhance the realism, add highlights in white. Finally, import the painting into a drawing program and convert it with the trace tool or trace it by hand with the freehand tool or Bézier curve tool.

Our next project will make use of intermediate tools and techniques to create a company logo.

Creating a company logo

Our second intermediate project is to create a company logo. This is a departure from our previous projects in the sense that it is more of an experiment in using special effects than a drawing exercise. Logos typically require little drawing. Instead, they consist primarily of text, manipulated in some distinctive manner to impart a specific company image. The logo that we will create displays the company name, "WorldWide," in stretched letters mounted on an oval plaque, suggestive of a globe.

Our fourth sample project is to create this logo of raised text on a plaque.

The three main advantages of logos over other graphics are:

1.   They can be used repeatedly without any graphic alteration.

2.   They can be used in both formal and informal publications.

3.   They serve as graphic indications of a document's origin.

The best thing about creating a logo is that the process is often a one-time experience. Once finished, you can use a logo over and over again without fear of audience reproach. Though viewers naturally tire of multiple exposures to a standard illustration, they are conditioned to see the same logo repeatedly. Your readers may even come to expect at least one version of your logo in every document that you publish. Since logos can be used more often than any other type of graphic, even page ornaments, they are a great time investment.

A logo is also an incredibly versatile graphic. It can embellish any document, from an informal newsletter to a legal contract.

Finally, a logo can be used to indicate a publication's origin. For example, suppose your company is large enough to support many departments or locations. A slightly different logo can be assigned to each division.

 ACME®productions

 ACME®distributions

ACME®marketing

Different departments within the same company are commonly assigned slightly different logos. These logos can be used to graphically identify the origin of a publication.

Now to begin creating our logo: rather than sketching the logo, as we have begun projects in the past, we will begin working on the final output. The basic form of the logo is not complex enough to warrant a sketch.

Generally, the first step in creating a logo is to create the logo text. But before entering text from the keyboard, you may want to determine the type specifications by choosing typeface, style, size, and alignment commands. Change the font to Times; change the type style to bold; change the type size to 30-point; and change the alignment to center.

Next, select the type tool and click in the center of your screen. Since the text in our logo needs to be entirely in capital letters, press the caps lock key on your keyboard. Then enter the logo text: WORLDWIDE. Press the caps lock key again to disengage it, so that it will not affect the rest of the creation of our logo. (In some programs, the caps lock key will act like the shift key, constraining cursor movement when pressed.) If your program provides a dialog box for entering text, click the OK button to display the text on the page.

WORLDWIDE

Your text should look like this if properly set in centered 30-point Times bold. The specific placement of text block handles varies from software to software.

As we discussed in *The type tool and font commands* section of Chapter 3, text in most drawing programs is just another graphic element that can be transformed and manipulated. In this case, we want to stretch the text block to twice its current height without changing its width in order to give the letters a condensed appearance.

The method for scaling your text block depends on your software. In many programs, you may drag upward on the text block's top transformation handle, or downward from the bottom handle. In other programs, you may use a special scaling tool. In either case, enlarge the text to 200% vertically.

If your software offers a "Horizontal scaling" option, you may achieve the same effect by changing the type size to 60-point and specifying a horizontal scaling of 50%.

WORLDWIDE

Stretch the text block to twice its normal height to give it a condensed appearance.

If your software is not capable of scaling type, leave the text block as it is and follow along with the rest of the project as usual.

In the picture of the finished logo at the beginning of this section, you will notice that in addition to appearing raised, the letters appear to be surrounded by a slight shadow that enhances the appearance of depth. For simplicity's sake, we will create this shadow first and then layer the raised effect in front of it.

The shadow is slightly gradated. From our discussion of stroking effects (in Chapter 4), we know that a gradated shadow can be the result of applying increasingly darker and thinner strokes to multiple text blocks. To start, stroke this text block with a 5-point line weight whose color is defined as a 15% black tint. The fill doesn't matter, since it will be covered by cloned text blocks, so leave it black.

Next, clone the text block, position the clone directly in front of the original, and stroke it with a 25% black, 4-point line weight.

Clone this text block and stroke the newest clone with a 35% black, 3-point line weight. The result of our stroking effect is shown below.

When previewed or printed, your shadow effect will appear as shown above. So far it looks like a big mess, but we've just begun.

Now we will add the raised text effect. Once again, this is accomplished by adding stroked clones in front of our current text blocks. Select the front text block, clone it again, and position the clone directly in front of the other text blocks. Stroke this type with 100% black, 2-point line weight.

Clone the forward text block again, but this time move it 1 point up and 1 point to the left of the other text blocks. This slight offset will give the logo its raised appearance. Fill this clone with solid white, and delete its stroke.

By applying the layer-and-offset method described in Chapter 4, we created the raised type effect shown above.

That's all there is to making the text. If you're unhappy with the letter spacing, you may want to kern some of the characters, but otherwise, we're ready to move on to the plaque.

The following step is the only real drawing you will have to perform in this project. Select the oval tool and draw an ellipse that surrounds the text, as shown below. The type should appear centered inside the ellipse. Also, leave about a half inch of space between the left and right sides of the ellipse and the sides of the text block.

Draw an oval completely surrounding the text blocks with a half inch to spare on each side.

That's enough drawing for one sample project. Now it's time to get back to the stroking effects. Stroke the ellipse with a 15% black, 5-point line weight, the same stroke we applied to the rear text block. Also apply a solid black fill.

Next, clone the ellipse, position the clone directly in front of the original, and stroke it with a 25% black, 4-point line weight. (Is this beginning to sound familiar?)

To finish the shadow effect, clone the ellipse again and stroke the newest clone with a 35% black, 3-point line weight. The result of our stroking effect is shown below.

When previewed or printed, the elliptical shadow effect will appear as shown above. The type is no longer visible, being hidden for now behind the ovals.

We will create the raised plaque a little differently than we did the raised text. First, clone the front ellipse, again position it directly in front of the others, and stroke this type with a 100% black, 2-point line weight.

In the picture of the finished logo at the beginning of this section, the plaque is bordered by heavy black crescents on each side, giving it a beveled appearance. To create this effect, the foremost ellipse must be reduced in width. Clone the newest ellipse and scale the clone to roughly 90% horizontally. Be careful to scale the ellipse with reference to its center, or you'll have to reposition it when you're finished.

Now offset the reduced ellipse. As with the text block, move it up 1 point and to the left 1 point. Then fill it with solid white and delete the stroke. The result is shown below.

When previewed or printed, the plaque will appear as shown above. By reducing the width of the offset shape, we have created a beveled effect.

The last step is to send the plaque in back of the text. Select all five ovals that make up the plaque and choose "Send to back" or an equivalent command. If you're having difficulty selecting all the ovals without selecting text blocks as well, you may send each ellipse to back individually, starting with the foremost ellipse and working backward.

The logo is now finished. If you like, you can add some additional details. Unlike previous projects, however, we warn you to use moderation when embellishing a logo. Most successful logos are very simple. The following figures display a couple of enhancement possibilities that improve the appearance of our logo without undermining its utility.

The subtle addition of a trademark indicates that we're serious about our logo and the company that it represents. If the company name is a registered trademark, add an ®, which can be accessed by pressing option-R.

In this example, we apply a slight gradation, starting at 15% black, fading to white, and then fading back to 15% black. The gradation enhances the depth of the logo, making the beveled plaque appear more realistic.

This completes our drawing of a company logo. You should save the logo to disk if you have not done so already. As always, you may print your logo or combine it with other text and graphic elements in a page-layout or presentation program.

This ends our fourth sample project. We have demonstrated how to create an abstract form about a central text block, how to stretch type, and how to use special stroking effects to create shadows, raised type, and beveled ellipses.

Logos are among the most useful graphics, due to their longevity, their versatility, and their quick distribution of information. In general, we recommend that a logo accompany every document that you produce, whether it appears as a boxed item at the bottom of a page or as a personal letterhead.

In this sample project, we have designed and executed a logo. When you create a logo, however, you may work from an existing design, either converting it to an electronic environment or embellishing it to represent the identity of your specific department. In either case, the approach is the same—the type is always the central graphic object.

The following chapter contains an additional sample project at an advanced level of difficulty. If you feel that you have successfully completed the previous projects and understand the techniques, tools, and commands covered, you will probably have little difficulty in moving on to the next chapter. If you feel unsure of any point that we have covered, or are not satisfied with your work, you may want to re-examine Chapters 1 through 4, or perhaps try out some sample projects of your own.

An Advanced Hands-On Project

CHAPTER 7

This chapter is the last of three chapters that provide step-by-step explanations of the creation of specific graphics using a drawing application. We discuss each of the features and methods introduced in Chapters 1 through 4 while working toward an actual goal. All projects are "hands-on," demonstrating how to create free-form computer artwork according to easy-to-follow, concise guidelines.

In this chapter, we will create a single advanced-level graphic: a realistically rendered, voluminous object. This project concentrates on the most difficult aspects of graphic composition. If you have not yet completed the graphics in the previous two chapters, we advise you to at least read through them at this time. By becoming familiar with the techniques, tools, and commands covered in Chapters 5 and 6, you will be more prepared to create the complex graphic examined in this chapter.

As we have advised in the last two chapters, you should not expend too much effort trying to match your graphic to ours dot-for-dot. Realism can be interpreted by different artists in many different ways, so it is increasingly important that you try to work your own style into this final project. By following our general directions in a manner that seems comfortable to you, you may learn personal drawing habits that will be helpful when you create artwork in the future.

Creating a voluminous object

Our advanced project is to create a realistic drawing of an everyday object—in this case, a lamp. This graphic concentrates exclusively on the drawing process with no attention to special effects. Though this project may prove challenging, our approach to it simplifies the process so that you should be able to complete the drawing with very satisfactory results.

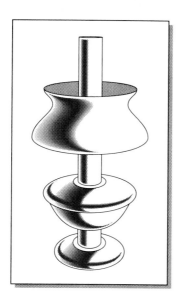

Our fifth sample project is to create this realistic image of a lamp with spherical parts.

Well-executed, realistic drawings are useful in every publication. Therefore, regardless of your subject matter, a realistic drawing approach is always acceptable. However, creating a realistic drawing also consumes more time and energy than creating other types of drawings, so you will probably want to pursue realism only when it is absolutely necessary. Realism is generally absolutely imperative only under the following circumstances:

1. When creating a portrait to accompany an article about a person for promotional or informational purposes.

2. When rendering an illustration of a product distributed by your company.

3. When the subject of a story is serious in nature. The most serious subjects can generally best be rendered realistically.

Creating a stylized graphic for any of these topics might make your publication less effective.

Each of the three types of drawing shown above—portrait, product illustration, and serious-subject graphic—require a realistic drawing approach.

The first thing you will notice about this sample project is that we concentrate less on tools, commands, and patterns than on drawing techniques. We assume you now understand how to operate each tool and how to perform common transformations. If you are unclear about any tool or transformation used in this project, refer to Chapters 3, 5, and 6 for more information.

The graphic building block that is most instrumental in turning a well-executed form into a realistic graphic is *volume*, which includes origin of light and shadow. These techniques were introduced in Chapter 2; we will demonstrate them in this project. In addition, we will utilize a bit of perspective technique in order to create our sketch.

In each of the previous projects, our sketch has been simple, and we have used it only to provide a basic framework we then carefully manipulated to create the final graphic. The sketch for this illustration is more involved, requiring several steps to complete. In fact, it is difficult to distinguish where the sketch ends and where the actual drawing begins when creating a realistic illustration. The entire project can be looked at as a series of sketches, one built on top of another until the drawing takes on a finished appearance.

Because our lamp has spherical shapes, taking a cross section of any portion of it—base, body, stem, or shade—will produce a perfect circle. With this in mind, we will begin the sketch of our lamp as a series of circles, displayed at different perspectives.

The first step is to draw an oval about two inches wide and one inch tall, although the dimensions are not important. Think of this oval as a circle displayed at a random perspective, representing a typical cross section from the lamp. Then select this shape and create four clones in vertical alignment with the original oval, spaced about one-quarter inch from each other. We will use each of these five ovals to represent a key cross section of the lamp.

Each cross section must be represented at a slightly different perspective to give our lamp an impression of depth. To imitate this perspective, we will stretch or compress each oval vertically. Select the bottom oval and stretch it to 130% vertically. We'll skip the second-to-bottom oval, since its perspective is acceptable. Then select the middle oval, and reduce it to 70% vertically. Reduce the second-to-top oval to 40% vertically, and reduce the top oval to 10% vertically. The width of each oval should remain unchanged.

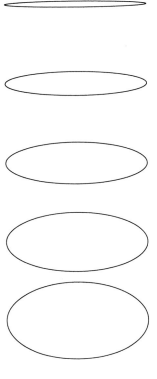

Each of our five ovals is displayed at a different perspective, representing cross sections of our lamp. Notice that the top oval has been squished to the point that it's barely more than a horizontal line.

A stem runs through the center of the lamp. This stem starts inside the base, pierces the body of the lamp, and ends at the top oval. To create a path for the stem, clone the bottom oval, reduce it to 25% proportionally, and position it in the upper portion of the original oval. Repeat this operation on the second-to-bottom oval. Also scale the top oval to 25% about the center of the shape. (Do not clone the top oval before scaling it.)

Other ovals need to be scaled as well, since not all of the lamp's parts are the same width. The middle oval represents the bottom of the lampshade, so it needs to be enlarged to 125% proportionally. The bottom oval is the base of the lamp, so reduce it to 75%. For both transformations, scale about the center of the shape.

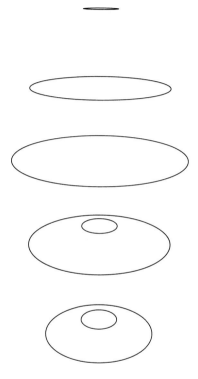

Scale the top oval and create smaller clones inside the bottom two ovals to represent cross sections of the stem. We also scale the second-to-top and bottommost ovals proportionally to more accurately represent the cross sections of the lamp.

The five main ovals shown above represent, from top to bottom, the top of the stem, the top of the lampshade, the bottom of the lampshade, the top of the body of the lamp, and the base. We will now connect these shapes to make them more recognizable.

Using the line tool or polygon tool, draw a vertical line extending from the right side of the topmost oval to the right side of the small, bottom oval. This line represents the right side of the lamp stem.

Then, draw in the right side of the lampshade and the right side of the body using the freehand tool or the more precise Bézier curve tool.

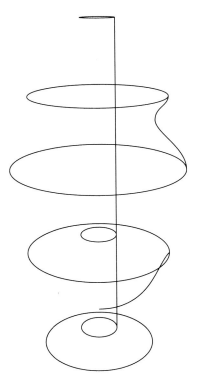

Draw in the right edges of the stem, lamp shade, and body of the lamp.

The reason we drew only the right edges of the various portions of the lamp is because the lamp is symmetrical; we can flip the right edges horizontally to represent the corresponding left edges. Select the vertical line and the two free-form paths that represent the right edges of the lamp. Clone all three paths and flip them horizontally. Then drag them into place to form the left edges of the lamp.

The two small ovals surrounding the lamp stem are the inner edges of two rings. To create each outer edge, clone a small oval and enlarge the clone to 140% about its center. Then offset each clone 1 point downward, so that each outer ring is a little off center. This offset will enforce the three-dimensional appearance of the lamp.

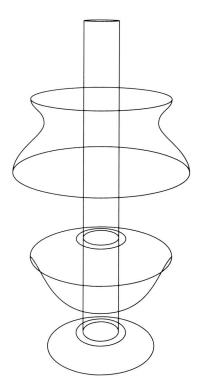

Flip clones of the right edges of the lamp and add two rings around the stem to complete the basic outline of the lamp.

Our present lamp appears to be made of glass. We can see through the shade to the stem, through the stem to the base, and so on. To make the lamp seem like a solid, physical object, we will connect various lines to build shapes. We will then fill and layer these shapes to cover overlapping lines.

For example, to close the lamp shade, you need to create two shapes, one to represent the front of the shade and the other to represent the back. First, separate the oval at the top of the shade into two halves, upper and lower. Similarly separate the oval at the bottom of the lamp shade. Then delete the top half of the lower oval.

Join the bottom point of the path on the left side of the lamp shade with the left point in the bottom half of the lower oval. Then join the right point in the bottom half of the lower oval with the bottom point of the path on the right side of the lamp shade. The result will be a single, open path that forms the left, bottom, and right sides of the lamp shade. Copy this path. Then join both ends of this path with the left and right points in the top half of the upper oval. Send the resulting shape to back and fill it with a light black tint. Paste the path you just copied and join both ends of this path with the left and right points in the bottom half of the upper oval. Bring this closed path to front and fill it with white. The lamp shade now appears to surround the stem.

If your software doesn't allow you to break paths apart and join them together, you will have to trace the front and back shapes of the lamp shade (shown in the following figure) using the freehand tool.

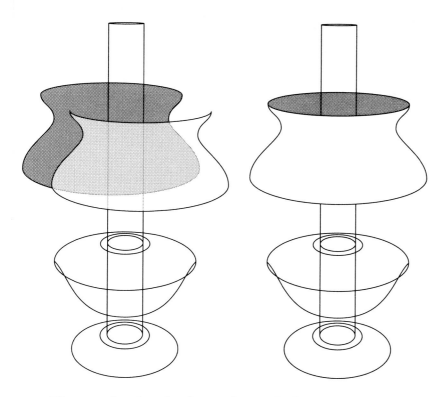

The two closed paths that make up the lamp shade are shown on the left. We have moved the forward shape slightly to make it appear transparent. When the two shapes are combined, they form a single lamp shade, as shown on the right.

We will create a few of the other objects in the lamp similarly, by breaking paths and joining them with other paths to form closed shapes. Next, fill the shapes with white and layer them to obscure the desired portions of other shapes to simulate the appearance of a real lamp. The following figure shows the shapes you should create and the order in which each shape should be layered.

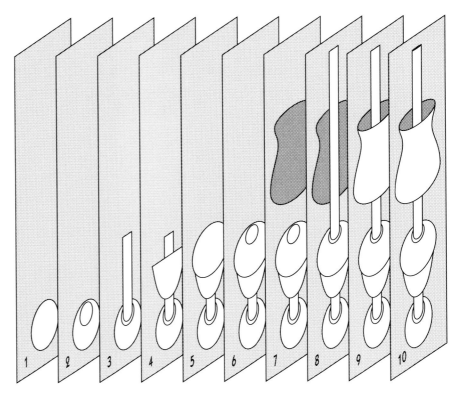

All in all, your paths must be disassembled and reassembled into ten shapes. Each shape should be layered in the order shown above, from back (1) to front (10).

Surprisingly little reshaping is required. For example, the first two shapes in the figure above are two ovals created during the sketch. They are used intact and require no reshaping. The third shape combines the innermost oval of the base with portions of the two lines that make up the stem. To create the fourth shape, we join the right and left paths that we drew to represent the body of the lamp. The fifth and sixth shapes are two more ovals used intact. The seventh and ninth shapes are the lamp shade paths we created on the previous page. The eighth shape combines the innermost oval of the body with portions of the two stem lines left over from the third shape. And the tenth shape is another intact oval; in this case, the extremely slender oval at the top of the stem.

Applying Your Knowledge

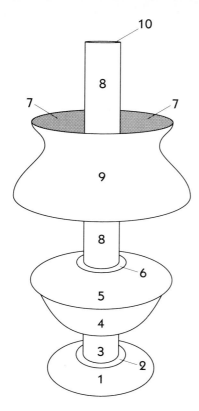

The completed lamp appears as shown above. Each shape is numbered in the order it is layered, from back to front. The two images labeled with a 7 are portions of the same shape, as are the two images labeled with an 8.

Having established the basic form of the lamp, you may, if you wish, consider this drawing finished. It is certainly adequate for many situations. For example, if you were creating an instruction manual for assembling a lamp, this straightforward drawing would be perfect. It displays all important elements of the lamp without including any unnecessary or confusing detail. However, the drawing is too flat or lackluster to be included as an element in a realistic illustration. To improve the realistic quality of the image, we will add shading.

Before we can determine how to shade an object, we must determine a light source. In our next figure, we have drawn a small sun to represent our light source. You can indicate yours simply as a circle. (Incidentally, we could have the lamp illuminate itself, as they often do, but we can achieve a more interesting result by utilizing an external light source.)

Once you have determined the location of your light source, sketch lines from the outer edges of the source to the surface of your lamp. These lines signify the angle at which light hits different portions of the lamp, helping you to determine where the lamp should be lit and where it should be unlit. We drew our lines using the line tool with a dashed stroke. Keep in mind that the light source and lines are for reference purposes only, so they don't need to look good. We will delete them before the drawing is finished.

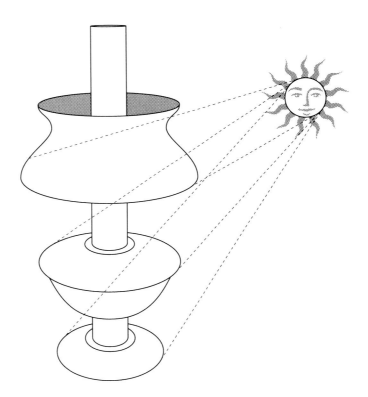

Indicate a light source and draw lines from it to key parts of the lamp.

Next, sketch the border lines between the lit and unlit areas of the lamp as shown in the figure below.

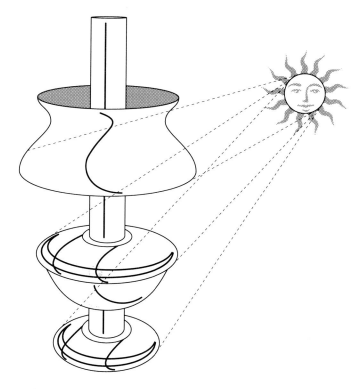

Draw lines to represent the borders between the lit and unlit portions of the lamp. We have applied a heavy stroke to our shading lines to distinguish them from the outlines of the lamp. Notice that the shadows cast by the stem onto the body and base of the lamp are parallel to the lines that emanate from the light source. Other lines, like those in the shade and stem, mimic the contour of the lamp.

After you finish sketching in the shading lines, delete the light source as well as the reference lines from the source to the lamp.

The sketch lines you have drawn indicate where shadows begin and end. To determine the exact shape of the shadows, you must join these beginning and ending lines to form closed paths. In some cases, you will simply have to join the lines to form shapes. In other cases, you will have to draw segments between lines to join them.

Once you complete the shadow shapes, delete their strokes and fill them with a light tint of black.

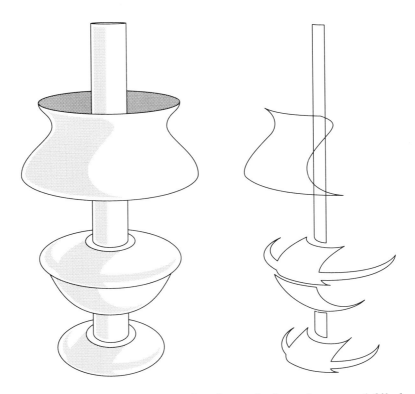

On the left, we have completed our shadow shapes and filled them with a 15% black tint. There are six paths in all, each of which is duplicated on the right with a thin stroke and no fill to better demonstrate its shape.

Applying Your Knowledge

The layering of your shadows is important. Each shadow should be layered directly in front of the shape upon which the shadow is cast. For example, the vertical shadow along the stem is layered in front of the stem itself. The shadow on the lamp shade is layered directly in front of the foremost lamp shade path.

We have again reached a possible stopping point. Our simple shadows indicate a light source and imply that the lamp has depth. However, if your software offers a gradation or blending feature, you may go one step further. Adding gradations to the shadow shapes will demonstrate the intensity of the light at various points on the lamp as well as suggest that all parts of the lamp are spherical.

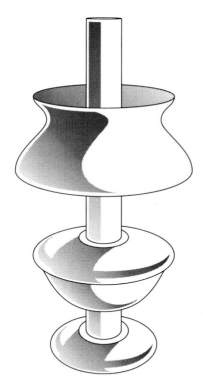

Add gradated shading to the lamp to enhance the sense of its volume. The above shading was created with an automatic gradation feature, as described on the following page.

If your software offers an automated gradation feature, fill all six shadow shapes with gradations that fade from 65% black to 15% black at an angle of 225° (down and to the left, which matches the direction of our light source lines). This ensures that the shadow is darkest at the point where it starts and lightest where it ends, as discussed in the *Reflection and reflected light* section of Chapter 2. You may also want to fill the rear lamp shade path with a gradation that progresses in the opposite direction (45°).

If your software offers a blending feature, you will be able to create a more realistic gradation, although it may require an extra 15 to 30 minutes of effort.

To create custom gradated shadows using a blending feature, you must first draw a path to represent the beginning color of each shadow. These beginning paths are shown above filled with dark tint of black.

Applying Your Knowledge

For each shadow, draw a path to represent the beginning color of the gradation, as shown in the previous figure. This path should contain the same number of points as the shadow path and should be layered directly in front of it. For best results, you may want to clone the shadow, scale it to a smaller size, and reshape it as desired. Then fill the new shapes with a 65% black tint.

Now use your software's blending feature to create a custom gradation between the beginning and ending color in the shadow. Use the blending tables at the end of Chapter 4 to determine the optimum number of steps to use.

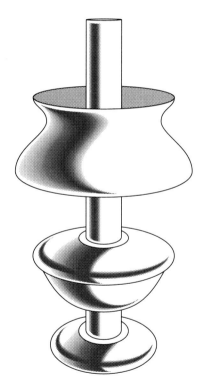

We blended each of the six shadows to produce the custom gradation shown above. These custom gradations appear more natural than the automated gradations of two figures ago.

This completes our drawing of a voluminous object. If you like, you can add a few small details or add or subtract some additional shading. You can even apply the fill-scale-and-skew method to add a shadow to define the surface on which the lamp rests, as described in Chapter 4.

Save the drawing to disk if you have not done so already. Then print your lamp image or combine it with text and graphics in a page-layout or presentation program.

———————◆◗◼◖◆———————

This ends our advanced sample project. We have demonstrated how to create a realistic form using volume, light, and shadow. We have also shown how to determine the perspective of an object during the first stages of a sketch, how to determine a light source, how to sketch the border between the lit and unlit areas of an object, and how to build up the shading of an object using gradations and blending.

Realistic illustrations are the most useful, versatile, and effective graphics that you can create, but they are also the most difficult and time-consuming. For this reason, you will probably want to limit your use of realism to necessary situations—portraits, product illustrations, and graphics for serious subjects. You should always keep in mind that silhouettes are much easier to create than voluminous objects and often satisfy many of the same publication requirements.

Enhancing Existing Artwork

P A R T

3

CHAPTER 8

Using clip-Art

In previous chapters, we have discussed how you can combine a knowledge of drawing theory with an understanding of software tools to develop a successful drawing technique in order to create both simple and sophisticated illustrations. We have focused on skills that will be helpful to you in creating custom drawings on your own, for your own purposes, from beginning to end.

But you don't always have to start from scratch. One advantage of electronic art is that it becomes a commodity of sorts. For example, you can make copies of all your artwork and trade it for an equal quantity of a fellow computer artist's work. This doubles your collection without requiring you to expend any extra effort. Now you have twice the resources on hand any time you begin a new graphic process, as described in Chapter 1. A sizable library of artwork frees you to spend less time sketching idea so that you can spend more time developing your technique and creating more sophisticated finished graphics.

One popular way to collect electronic drawings is to purchase *clip-art*—libraries of graphics sold commercially. Clip-art existed well before desktop publishing became popular. Most newspapers, for example, subscribe to monthly collections of clip-art in the form of tabloid magazines that contain several pages of camera-ready artwork. These graphics can be used for advertisements or editorial illustrations without paying royalties or hiring artists to render new images. The artwork tends to be generic in style as well as seasonal. In September, a clip-art collection may contain many back-to-school drawings. In October, you can expect to see pumpkins, ghosts, witches, and so on.

The best clip-art is applicable to a wide range of situations. For example, a single graphic might appear in the same issue of a newspaper in three different advertisements.

The best clip-art images are applicable to many different situations.

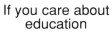
If you care about education

Vote YES on Amendment #3

A single clip-art image may satisfy many graphic requirements.

The advantage of clip-art sold on a disk over traditional clip-art packaged in a magazine is that it can be more easily and more thoroughly customized. After all, a clip-art graphic will rarely satisfy your requirements exactly. Even if you're fortunate enough to own a large supply of clip-art and organized enough to go through what you have available in a reasonable amount of time, you'll be lucky to find a graphic that almost meets your needs. Sometimes owning clip-art can be like subscribing to cable TV: despite a selection of more than 40 channels, how often do you find something you really want to watch? But unlike cable TV, clip-art can be altered to more specifically match your tastes.

If a traditional layout artist at a newspaper needs to modify a piece of camera-ready clip-art , he or she must first shoot a copy of the art using a photocopier or a camera to avoid ruining the original. If any special effects such as inverting or resizing are required (few other transformations are possible), they must be accomplished during the photographic cycle by a qualified camera person. The layout artist then performs detailed alterations using pen, ink, and a white-out liquid. Finally, the finished art is cut and pasted into place. The entire process is expensive and limiting, demanding tight organization and a patient production manager. By contrast, electronic clip-art was invented to be modified.

Of course, you can use a piece of clip-art just as you find it. Sometimes, a purchased graphic suits a situation exactly. But generally, we find modification to be an instrumental step toward using clip-art to adequately enhance your documentation.

Unlike traditional clip-art, electronic clip-art can be easily and thoroughly customized.

Modification is
an instrumental
step toward
using clip-art to
enhance your
documentation.

You can easily modify electronic clip-art to meet any graphic requirement. From start to finish, the above modification took about 30 minutes. We would have been better off starting from scratch if we had to perform the same modification by hand.

This chapter addresses three methods for manipulating clip-art:

1. How to customize clip-art to exactly meet your needs.

2. How to combine multiple clip-art images.

3. How to mix clip-art images with your original drawings.

This chapter contains no advice regarding the purchasing of clip-art, nor is it a catalog of available clip-art. We merely provide assistance for using clip-art. Considering the hundreds of clip-art packages available, we must leave the choice of purchases to you. An appendix contains a list referencing the origin of each graphic used in our text along with vendor information. However, this is by no means a complete list of what's available; we include it only to give credit where credit is due.

Enhancing Existing Artwork

Customizing clip-art

You can easily modify electronic clip-art to exactly meet your graphic requirements. We will prove this by demonstrating some of the most simple methods for enhancing clip-art—methods that produce dramatic results, yet require little time or energy.

Simple clip-art transformations

Sometimes the simplest transformations can change a piece of inadequate clip-art into precisely the graphic you've been looking for. Clip-art can be scaled, flipped, rotated, slanted, colored, and so on, just like any other image in a drawing program. This fact is often overlooked by people who want to improve their documentation, but hesitate to alter clip-art for fear of ruining it. Fortunately, you don't need much artistic sensibility to perform a small transformation that can change the attitude of an image without adversely affecting the precision of its form.

You don't need much artistic sensibility to perform a small transformation on a clip-art image.

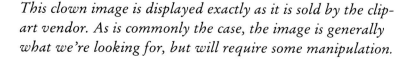

This clown image is displayed exactly as it is sold by the clip-art vendor. As is commonly the case, the image is generally what we're looking for, but will require some manipulation.

*Here we have deleted the dog, the balloons , and the ground,
and applied transformations. We rotated the first clown to
make him stand up straight. We rotated the second clown
even more to make him lean backward. We flipped the third
clown horizontally, moved all paths except his shoe upward,
and rotated his shoe to make him appear to be standing on
his toes.*

If a piece of clip-art doesn't exactly satisfy your requirements,
change it. Small changes can be especially effective, yet require almost
no time or talent.

Sometimes, a transformation can be accomplished by choosing a
single command. But some special effects, while no more difficult,
demand a little more time.

Modification hints and tips

In Chapter 4, we disclosed a series of tips: how to apply special line
effects, how to add a shadow to an image, and how to create seamless
gradations. Each of these special effects methods is as applicable to
clip-art as it is to your original artwork.

We have applied one of our hints and tips from Chapter 4 to each of the clowns above. We applied the layer-and-offset method to make the first clown appear raised from the page. We added a shadow to the second clown. And we consulted the blend tables at the end of Chapter 4 to determine the number of steps with which to fill the third clown.

Any tip explained in Chapter 4 may be used to enhance a clip-art image.

In this sense, our special effects tips are really just extensions of the transformation features included with your drawing application. They are slightly more difficult to complete, but their results are more sensational.

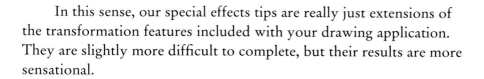

You can dramatically alter or enhance any piece of clip-art without drawing a single line, using your drawing program's built-in reshaping and transformation capabilities in addition to our special effects tips from Chapter 4. In the next two sections of this chapter, we discuss how to perform additional graphic enhancements by combining clip-art images with each other and with your own illustrations. The latter section explores how to use drawing theory to embellish a clip-art image.

Combining multiple clip-art images

When you were in grade school, perhaps you participated in an art project that involved clipping pictures from magazines and pasting these pictures into a collage. The most successful collage in the class was probably created by the student who was best at selecting and assembling images rather than by the student who excelled at drawing them from scratch. Creating a graphic using clip-art is likewise a process of collage. Your ability to successfully combine clip-art images will be determined by your ability to assemble images into a single, cohesive illustration.

When combining separate images, you must first consider how they will look together. Will they merge to form a single compatible illustration or will they look like two separate images that somehow got too close to each other? Generally, only images created in similar styles can be combined into a single harmonious graphic.

Determining similar clip-art styles

In Chapter 1, we discussed how you can develop your own personal artistic style to enhance the successfulness of your graphics. In the process of developing a style, you may integrate the styles of a variety of established artists, but ultimately your style must be your own.

So, in a sense, styles are like snowflakes; no two are identical. However, if you can pinpoint enough stylistic similarities between two images, then you may in turn combine the images into a cohesive whole. But, how can you recognize that two images have styles which are similar enough to be combined?

First, if two clip-art images appear to be created by the same artist, then they can be combined. This is because, theoretically, an artist has only one style.

Only images created in similar artistic styles should be combined into a single graphic.

Some clip-art vendors are very small. The fact that the desktop publishing industry has yet to fully grow out of its grass-roots origins means that there remains room for the little guy. It is not uncommon for an artist to single-handedly create and sell personal graphics as clip-art. Other vendors purchase images from only a handful of free-lance artists. You may therefore easily combine different pieces of clip-art obtained from small developers.

Images sold by small clip-art developers are often the work of a single artist.

Each of these musical instruments was drawn by the same artist. Since the artistic style of all five images is identical, they may be combined within a single illustration.

Unfortunately, as a market grows, the little guy either grows into a big guy or gets squeezed out entirely. This means small clip-art developers are becoming less and less popular. So in all probability, most clip-art you buy will originate from an art warehouse, a vendor who owns stockpiles of art collected over the years from literally hundreds of artists. Due to the stylistic differences of the many artists, your job of combining images is made more difficult.

Ultimately, you will have to experiment with combining art before you become fully knowledgeable about which styles work together and which do not. We can, however, provide some sample combinations of images that we think conflict with each other and combinations that blend to form seamless illustrations.

The following is a list of warnings about stylistic combinations that do not blend well together. Each warning is followed by two graphics, one that violates and one that obeys the rule.

1. Do not combine cartoon images with serious graphics.

Cartoon images rarely combine well with serious drawings.

One of these people is represented as a cartoon, the other is represented realistically. They do not combine well because of their stylistic differences.

Each of these people is represented in a similarly realistic style. Thus they combine well.

2. Do not combine geometric and naturalistic images.

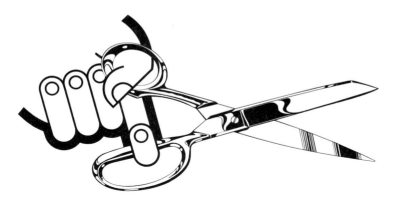

Geometric images and naturalistic drawings look strange together.

The hand has been executed in a very geometric style, while the scissors are rendered naturalistically. Because a viewer will recognize that the two objects are the creations of different artists, they appear awkward when combined into a single illustration.

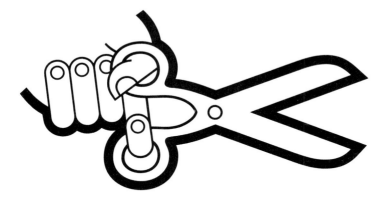

Here, we substitute a geometrically stylized pair of scissors for the naturalistic pair. By applying a thick outline to the entire image, we link the hand and scissors together. Incidentally, the scissors are actually a character from the Zapf Dingbats font enlarged to a 200-point type size and embellished with a special stroking effect.

3.   Do not combine "heavy" images with delicate line drawings.

Heavy images
tend to
overwhelm
delicate line
drawings.

The woman in this figure is a heavy image composed of many large black shapes and thick lines. By contrast, the man is delicate, the result of paths with thin strokes and no fills. The two appear as two separate objects placed beside each other, rather than blending to form a single illustration.

This drawing is composed almost entirely of paths with thin outlines. Although the physical relationship between the two images is rather fantastic, the images combine well because of their stylistic similarities.

Enhancing Existing Artwork

When combining different clip-art images, first determine whether the images share a similar astyle. Images drawn by the same artist may almost always be combined, but you must experiment with images created by different artists, ultimately judging for yourself whether they combine to produce a harmonious or disparate effect.

Matching similar styles is only part of the art of combining multiple clip-art images. After you find images that seem to be drawn in a similar style, you must determine how to position the images relative to each other.

Positioning multiple images to interact

Regardless of the stylistic similarities between two images, they will appear awkward next to each other unless they interact. After all, what purpose does a graphic serve if its objects have no obvious relationship to each other?

After you find images drawn in similar styles, you must determine how to position them relative to each other.

Although these elements have been drawn in an identical style, they seem to have no relationship to each other. No object relates to any other object; they are simply jumbled together like a graphic salad.

When considering whether to add a piece of clip-art to a graphic, make sure that you can graphically define its purpose. Each image should appear essential to the context of the illustration; none should appear to be just sitting around.

Sometimes clip-art images have to be altered or transformed before they can be placed in the same illustration. The building blocks of drawing theory that we discussed in Chapter 2 are just as relevant when using clip-art as they are for creating original drawings. Are objects scaled correctly in relation to each other? Should their proportions be altered in order to improve their interaction? Is the origin of light consistent from object to object? If theoretical problems do exist, use your drawing application's tools and commands to remedy the problems by changing the clip-art images.

One clip-art object must work with its fellow objects to form a complete illustration.

Here we have manipulated our collection of elements to form a cohesive illustration. Although no reshaping was required, we repositioned the images and scaled them to create more interesting size relationships.

Any method that is applicable to customizing clip-art images individually can be applied to creating relationships between various clip-art images. No clip-art object is an island; it must work with its fellow objects to form a complete illustration.

Combining clip-art is a way of creating full illustrations that involves less work than drawing from scratch. To successfully combine different clip-art images, you must integrate both an intuitive ability to create collage with a knowledge of clip-art customization, which we discussed earlier in this chapter. Images must match each other stylistically and interact to form a harmonious graphic.

Our final method for using clip-art explains how to combine a clip-art image with an original drawing to produce truly customized graphics.

Inserting clip-art into original drawings

A very complex illustration can rarely be assembled simply by combining existing images. Sometimes, no matter how thoroughly you search your clip-art library, you cannot locate that one object that will make your graphic successful. In such a case, you may have to partially draw the graphic on your own and combine it with clip-art to produce the finished piece.

When combining clip-art with your own work, you must take into account the same stylistic considerations we discussed for combining multiple clip-art images. In essence, either the clip-art must match your style or you must match the style of the clip-art.

When combining clip-art with your own work, the clip-art should match your style or you should draw in the style of the clip-art.

Finding clip-art similar to your personal style

When combining clip-art with your own art, you are always combining the work of two different artists. Hence, there will always be some discrepancy in style. But you can partially match your style by selecting clip-art similar to your own. In Chapter 1, we suggested that you develop your personal style by copying from the work of established artists. If you were forward-thinking enough to consult clip-art when developing your style, then you may be able to combine that clip-art with your own artwork to produce finished illustrations.

However, few of us even considered clip-art when developing a style. After all, clip-art is rarely produced by leading professionals in the art world. Despite clip-art's inestimable utility, consulting clip-art for artistic style is like consulting a discount house for this year's fashion trends. Clip-art is supermarket material, not "high art."

Clip-art often imitates the work of successful commercial artists or commercial art trends.

But just as an outfit you find in a department store is often an imitation of a successful fashion designer's work, clip-art often imitates the work of successful commercial artists or commercial art trends. This is because clip-art companies recognize that familiar-looking graphics sell well. When looking for clip-art that matches your style, you may therefore find it helpful to keep in mind the artists that you have imitated and keep an eye out for similar imitations in your clip-art library. If a clip-art image borrows from the same artist from whom you borrowed, your graphic and the clip-art will probably work together stylistically.

Matching clip-art style to your personal style is one way of combining clip-art with your own work to form a successful finished illustration. Look for artwork that seems to share common stylistic origins with your work.

In these days of Coolidge-like prosperity, you see many clip-art images reminiscent of 1920s poster art. If your personal artistic style is based on this genre of art as well, then this dancer based on a classic design from Fred H. Ball might combine well with your work.

Look for clip-art that appears to share stylistic origins with your artwork.

Another way to combine clip-art with your artwork requires less searching but more flexibility on your part. This method involves selecting any clip-art that suits your conceptual purpose, and modifying your style to match that of the clip-art when filling in missing details.

Modifying your style to match clip-art

Big graphic concepts require numerous graphic elements. Suppose that you want to create a pleasant city scene. If you're lucky, you can locate a complete city scene graphic from your clip-art library.

However, finished multi-object graphics are not very popular clip-art images, since uses for complex drawings are inherently more limited. In all probability, you will have to create the drawing from scratch or piece it together using several clip-art images—a few cars, a house, some people engaged in everyday activities, maybe even a few animals—tied together with details you fill in from scratch. You are unlikely to find such a variety of clip-art objects that match your personal artistic style; in fact, you will be hard-pressed to locate so many images that do not conflict with each other. But if you are able to herd together a generally compatible horde of objects, you will be better off altering your style to match that of the majority.

Matching a foreign style is not as difficult as you may think. Basically, you must observe the stylistic considerations we discussed in the *Combining multiple clip-art images* section, earlier in this chapter. Are the clip-art images cute or serious? Are they geometric or naturalistic? Are they heavy or delicate line drawings? After you have answered these questions, you can more accurately estimate how to modify your style.

When assembling a horde of compatible objects, alter your style to match that of the majority.

These consistently styled clip-art images offer a starting point for the creation of a city scene, but they are not enough to form a cohesive illustration on their own.

When
combining
several objects,
you often have
to add details
of your own
to complete
the illustration.

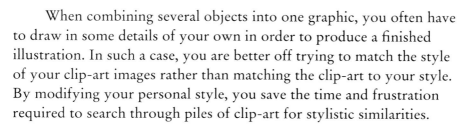

By manipulating the images from the previous figure and drawing several details in a matching style, we can create a full-blown illustration such as the intricate scene shown above.

When combining several objects into one graphic, you often have to draw in some details of your own in order to produce a finished illustration. In such a case, you are better off trying to match the style of your clip-art images rather than matching the clip-art to your style. By modifying your personal style, you save the time and frustration required to search through piles of clip-art for stylistic similarities.

The final issue regarding combining your drawings with existing art involves clip-art images that are designed to frame graphics or text rather than to serve as stand-alone illustrations. The following text explains how to use these clip-art borders, specifically in the context of framing your own work.

Framing your work with clip-art

Clip-art borders are becoming increasingly popular. They can be used to add a flourish to large book-cover text, to enhance advertisements, or to frame original illustrations.

Clip-art borders can be used to highlight text or frame graphics.

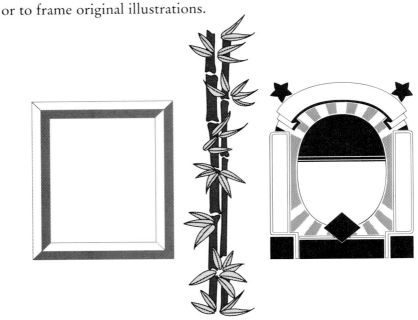

The variety of clip-art borders currently available spans simple lines to ornate floral designs to heavy frames.

Many clip-art vendors sell packages that contain borders exclusively. Although many are temptingly attractive, are they necessary? In fact, a successful graphic can stand alone quite adequately without a border. A border around a graphic is exactly like a frame around a painting in a gallery: it is an embellishment that succinctly defines the boundaries of the graphic. You already know where a painting ends simply by looking at it. But if you decide to add a border, based on personal preference, it can help to focus a viewer's attention on your work, separating the graphic from other elements on a page in a crisp, elegant manner.

When selecting a border, consider the character of the graphic it surrounds. A very heavy border can overpower a graphic; a very light border can be overpowered by the graphic.

A heavy border, which can overpower a graphic, is best reserved for framing type.

This illustration has a dense, geometric border. Although the image is strong and moderately heavy, the border competes with the artwork for viewer attention. This kind of border is best reserved for framing text.

An light or
delicate border
can be
overpowered
by the graphic.

*This border is too light for this image. It is so overwhelmed
by the illustration that it serves no purpose. Light borders
like this one are best for framing delicate line drawings.*

A heavy border should be used only with large, bold type. It
rarely lends itself to any but the heaviest of graphic elements. A light
border should be coupled primarily with medium-weight text or
delicate line drawings. Most drawings should receive a border that
consists of thick bold lines without exhibiting a conspicuous flam-
boyancy. A graphic frame should be weighty enough to support an
illustration, but not so pompous that it competes for viewer attention.

Consider your
border as just
another piece
of clip-art that
must be
balanced
with your
illustration.

This border suits our illustration much better than either of the previous examples. It is heavy enough to support the graphic, yet light enough to focus viewer attention on the graphic, not solely on itself. Notice also that the border matches the style and theme of the graphic.

Consider your border as simply another piece of clip-art that must be balanced with the rest of your original illustration. The frame should be stylistically compatible with your graphic.

Any two images, whether created by the same artist or not, must compliment each other stylistically when combined in a single illustration. So, when combining original work with purchased artwork, your must either locate clip-art that matches your style, or adjust your style to match that of the clip-art. This applies even to framing your work with a clip-art border. Borders serve primarily to define the boundaries of a graphic, but in a larger sense, they become an integral portion of the illustration. Every illustration is like a little country: Its parts may originate from many different backgrounds, but all must eventually blend together into a single stylistic melting pot.

Combining Objects with Scans

In the previous chapter, we discussed how you can build an illustration based on clip-art images collected or purchased from other artists. Clip-art provides a fundamental starting point in the graphic process, saving you the time-consuming task of creating illustrations from scratch.

Sometimes, however, you may want to base a drawing on an image that is not stored on disk, but exists on paper or as a photograph. In such a case, you may electronically *scan* the image; the scanning process is similar to photography in that you transfer the image from one environment to another. Electronic scans are produced using any of several compatible scanning devices, or *scanners*.

About scanners

Scanners are available in three varieties, including *hand-held*, *sheet-fed*, and *flat-bed*. To operate a hand-held scanner, you drag the device, with its sensor window facing down, over a desired image. A tracking roller on the bottom of the scanner ensures that the scanned image is proportional to the original, regardless of the speed at which you move the scanning device. Unfortunately, if your movements are crooked or choppy, the quality of your scan will suffer. Although several attempts are generally required to produce a perfect scan, a hand-held scanner allows you to scan images from books without photocopying or ripping out pages.

Scanners are available in monochrome, gray scale, and full-color models, increasing respectively in price.

If you are using a sheet-fed scanner, you load the hard copy image—preferably a photocopy rather than original artwork—into the device much as you would load a sheet of paper into a typewriter. The scanner then feeds the page through its rollers, scanning the image as the device's optic sensor sweeps back and forth in horizontal passes. But because pages sometimes misfeed and slippage is a constant annoyance, sheet-fed scanners are the least reliable scanning devices.

To operate a flat-bed scanner, you simply lay the page face down on the device window much as you would when operating a photocopier. The page remains stationary while the optic sensor moves sweep by sweep to record the image. Because this configuration allows the least room for human or hardware error, flat-bed scanners are typically the scanning devices of choice.

An additional distinction between scanners is color capability. Scanners are available in monochrome (black and white only), gray-scale (recording 16 to 256 shades of gray), and full-color models, increasing respectively in price.

Enhancing Existing Artwork

Today's inexpensive scanning technology can yield surprisingly accurate results.

All these images were scanned with a hand-held scanner capable of capturing 16 shades of gray. Although the images fall short of magazine-quality photographs, they demonstrate that inexpensive technology can yield surprisingly accurate and attractive results.

A scanner allows you to create electronic copies of original artwork and photographs. You may also scan photographs clipped from magazines or other periodicals, as well as classical artwork, maps, charts, and so on. Precaution should be exercised, however, since the copying of published images is often prohibited by copyright laws. You are better off scanning only those images which you know to be in the public domain or whose copyrights have expired, or images specifically commissioned by you or your company.

Enhancing scanned images

Regardless of the device used to capture it, a scanned image is always bitmapped. If you want to edit the pixels in a scanned image—such as changing the color of the bear or removing President Taft's hat in the previous figure—you must use the software provided with your scanner or, better yet, a color painting or photo-editing program. Most drawing programs, on the other hand, do *not* allow you to edit the pixels in a color bitmap.

You may use a high-end drawing program to embellish a gray-scale or color scan.

So how do you use scans in a drawing program? Well, for one thing, you may convert a scan into a series of object-oriented paths using your software's trace tool, as we discussed in Chapter 3. Or, if you prefer, you may trace the scanned image by hand using the freehand, polygon, or Bézier curve tool.

But you will rarely want to trace a scanned image that includes colors or shades of gray. After all, why trace a piece of artwork when it looks fine as it is? Although bitmapped, the images in the previous figure don't appear particularly jagged. The fact that neighboring pixels are colored in similar shades of gray disguises the borders between pixels to create a consistent, photographic image.

So rather than tracing color scans, you may prefer to embellish them. Many drawing programs allow you to manipulate bitmaps using standard transformation features.

Transforming scans

In many drawing programs, an imported scan may be subjected to any transformation that is applicable to, say, a geometric object. Obviously, this includes selecting, moving, deleting, or layering a scan. However, you may also be able to scale, flip, rotate, or skew it.

Scans can be transformed in a drawing program without sacrificing the resolution of the image.

Shown above are stretched, flipped, rotated, and skewed versions of the photograph of President Taft.

In transforming a bitmap, your software transforms the shape of each and every pixel in the image. For example, each of the pixels in the stretched image above has been stretched into a tall rectangle. The pixels in the skewed image have been slanted. As a result, you may transform scanned images without sacrificing resolution.

You may use one or more transformed scans to create perspective effects, such as billboards or photographic cubes. An example of this is shown on the following page.

You may use transformed scans to create perspective effects, such as this cube.

Transformed scans can be combined to create familiar images. This photo box was created by scaling, rotating, and skewing three scans and adding a gradated shadow.

Unfortunately, a transformed scan is a lot like transformed type; it looks great the first few times around, but its appeal becomes dated surprisingly quickly. If you use transformations excessively, your artwork will start looking like a bad 1960s film with split screens. Luckily, there are better ways to manipulate scans in a drawing program.

Adding objects to scanned backgrounds

Object-oriented images are smooth and crisp, often more real than life. A computer illustration tends to appear if it is being viewed at an impossibly high level of focus. But as we discussed in the *Demonstrating depth* section of Chapter 2, an image should appear in focus only

Enhancing Existing Artwork

if it is part of the foreground. In real life, background images appear slightly hazy or blurred. Out-of-focus images are nearly impossible to create using paths, strokes, and fills. Scanned images, however, are more naturalistic. Though not inherently less focussed than drawings, scans typically appear softer and more mellow than a collection of precise, object-oriented lines and shapes. Therefore, a scan may serve as the perfect backdrop for a drawing.

Here we have combined a piece of clip art with a scan of a hotel interior. The result is a pleasant contrast between line art and photography. The fan motifs help to define the borders of the image.

A scanned interior or landscape may be the perfect backdrop for an object.

For best results, an object positioned in front of a scanned background should be filled with dark colors.

Scanned images tend to be dense. A scanned background will overpower your foreground object unless the object is equally dense. Also, your foreground object should be darker than the scanned background. In the previous figure, the woman is drawn in black. The pixels in the scan have been lightened to appear farther away. (See the *Shades of depth* discussion in Chapter 2.) Some drawing applications offer image control features that allow you to lighten or darken a scanned image or adjust the amount of contrast between pixels. If your software does not provide such a feature, you may lighten the scanned image in a color painting application before importing it into your drawing program.

The next two methods for combining scans with objects involve actually integrating scans into the form of the object. In the following discussion, we discuss how to use a scanned image as a tile pattern. After that, we examine how to mask a scanned image.

Scanned tile patterns

A few drawing applications permit you to integrate scans into tile patterns. Begin with a small scanned image, like one of the heads from Picasso's *Les Demoiselles D'Avignon*, shown in the first figure in this chapter. Then repeat the image throughout a shape, as described in the *Creating textural patterns* section of Chapter 3.

If your software does not allow you to use scans in a tile pattern, you may create your pattern before importing it. Using a color painting or photo-editing application, select the image you want to use as the tile and clone it repeatedly to create a horizontal strip of tiles. Then select the entire strip and clone it again and again, vertically. Next import it into your drawing program and mask it with a path. If your program does not provide an automated masking feature, use the cookie-cutter method described in Chapter 4.

In some software, a small scanned image may be used as a tile in a fill pattern.

The primary shape in the top image is a complicated black path that defines the outline of the hair and glasses of the woman's head. (Several small white paths are layered in front of this shape to provide detail.) Large shapes are easily integrated with scans. In the lower image, we have filled the large image with a scanned pattern to produce a surrealistic, mesmerizing effect.

Another way to integrate scans into object-oriented paths is to use your program's masking feature. A moment ago, we mentioned how masking can be used to fill an image with a scanned pattern. Now, we will discuss how it can be used to smooth the outline of a bitmapped image.

Masking scans

Suppose you want to extract a detail from a scanned image. If you erase the extraneous images inside a color paint program, the remaining detail will appear to have jagged edges, due to the harsh contrast between the outline of the image and the empty background. So rather than erasing unwanted elements, mask them in a drawing program.

Trace a path around the image you want to keep using the freehand or Bézier curve tool. Then apply your program's "Mask" feature or use the cookie-cutter method described in Chapter 4. Stroke the mask with a thin, black outline to highlight its smooth outline.

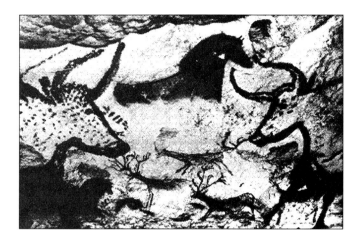

Masking a scanned image with an object-oriented path provides a smooth outline for the scan.

The first image is a photograph of the famous Lascaux cave paintings in southern France. Below that, we have masked away all but the right-hand bull as an element in a logo. Notice that the outline of the scanned bull is perfectly smooth, thanks to the thin stroke around the path.

Enhancing Existing Artwork

The smooth, precise outline that results from masking gives a scanned image a decidedly unrealistic appearance, as if the image has been clipped from a photograph. This effect is perfect for logos and other abstract drawing categories. However, if you would prefer a more naturalistic outline, you will have to use tools found in a color painting or photo-editing program to smear the edges.

Anything you can open or import into a drawing program may be refined, enhanced, or altered.

Anything that you can open or import into a drawing application—original artwork, clip-art, or scanned artwork or photographs—may be refined, enhanced, or simply altered to your specifications. The fact that you don't always have to start from scratch when creating an illustration is the real advantage of using computer graphics. Even people who aren't necessarily interested in drawing can learn to manipulate existing artwork to their satisfaction.

Scanned images can be traced, transformed, used as backgrounds, or integrated into the interiors of objects using a high-end drawing program. As always, the success of your implementation of these methods will rely on your knowledge of drawing theory and drawing tools. With enough experimenting, you will undoubtedly develop additional ways to manipulate scans.

Our final chapter reviews every drawing application presently available for Macintosh computers. Each review states whether the application allows you to import scanned artwork and what capabilities are available for editing the scan.

Software Review

CHAPTER 10

Drawing Programs on the Mac

In previous chapters, we have discussed how to create both simple and sophisticated illustrations using a typical drawing application. In this chapter, we concentrate entirely on the specific applications themselves. We review six drawing programs, all of which run on the Macintosh computer. Some of them, like MacDraw, are straightforward applications, offering only the most basic features covered in this book. Others, such as Adobe Illustrator and Aldus FreeHand, are high-end programs that run the whole gamut, allowing you to duplicate just about every figure in this book, from cover to cover.

Each review is made up of five parts:

1. *Introduction*

An introduction to the program, often including a brief history and any special features of the software.

2. *Hardware requirements*

The minimum system configuration required to run this application.

3. *Distinguishing features*

Features of this application that distinguish it from other applications. Most features are merely variations from the norm described in Chapter 3, but a few are exceptional features not covered in this book. The features are grouped by topics, which correspond to the topics discussed in Chapter 3:

- **Ⓐ** Opening and saving files

- **Ⓑ** Geometric tools

- **Ⓒ** Free-form tools and their operation

- **Ⓓ** Trace feature, as well as sensitivity adjustments for trace and freehand tools

- **Ⓔ** Reshaping free-form paths and geometric paths, including the insertion and deletion of points

- **Ⓕ** Transformations, including moving and layering; duplication; and scaling, flipping, rotating, and skewing

- **Ⓖ** Type, including spell checking (if available)

- **Ⓗ** Stroking and filling, including cap and join options, dash patterns, tile-patterned fills, masks, and gradations

- **Ⓧ** Miscellaneous features

Throughout the chapter we will use the circled letter icons shown on the previous page to highlight discussions of corresponding topics.

4. *Deviations from the norm*

Features that differ from those that are usually included in drawing software. Some items listed are simply inconsistencies within the program; however, many items genuinely curtail your drawing capabilities.

5. *Who needs this application?*

All in all, every one of these applications serves a legitimate purpose. But no software is for everyone. Here, we try to isolate what aspects of the application might specifically meet your requirements. This paragraph is specially designed for readers who are interested in purchasing drawing software.

For each application, we have included a graphic that displays one or more effects from the *Distinguishing features* list. And, of course, the name, address, and phone number of the product vendor is listed, along with the application's retail price tag. The version number of the application on which the review is based is listed under the price. These are the most recent versions available upon publication of this book, but since books tend to have long shelf lives, new versions may be available by the time you read this. We recommend you call vendors for complete information.

At the top outer corner of each page is the icon of the software being reviewed, so that you may easily locate a specific product by flipping through pages.

The following pages review the six finest drawing applications available for the Macintosh in alphabetical order. Scores or ratings are not included.

Adobe Illustrator

Adobe Systems made its first splash in the world of desktop publishing in 1985 when Apple debuted the LaserWriter. In the years since, it has become increasingly obvious that the typesetting industry was transformed almost overnight by the introduction of the PostScript language and its brand of object-oriented technology. Unfortunately, no software sufficiently addressed PostScript's true power to combine complex text and graphics on the printed page. This encouraged many computer artists to experiment with ways to create special effects by writing PostScript routines of their own. So in 1987, Adobe introduced Illustrator, an elegant product that managed to present the idea of Bézier curve handling in a package so intuitive that users fed up with the limitations of programs like MacDraw and SuperPaint could sink their teeth into it immediately. Illustrator has continued to dominate the free-form graphics market ever since.

Hardware requirements

- Macintosh Plus
- two Mbytes of RAM
- 20 Mbyte hard drive

Distinguishing features

- ❶ opens native PostScript files only
- ❶ imports MacPaint and EPS files
- ❶ saves in PostScript, EPS Mac, and EPS PC formats
- ❷ geometric path tools: rectangle and oval tools
- ❷ to display dialog and enter dimension and rounded corner radius specifications, click with rectangle tool

Distinguishing features (cont.)

- Ⓒ free-form path tools: freehand tool and fully functioning Bézier curve tool (pen tool)
- Ⓒ undraw mistakes with freehand tool by dragging with tool while pressing command key
- Ⓓ click with trace tool to create one path at a time
- Ⓓ freehand tolerance determines sensitivity of both freehand and trace tools
- Ⓔ use arrow tool to select and reshape paths; select path to display points and Bézier control handles
- Ⓔ to edit geometric shapes, first ungroup
- Ⓔ to insert point into path, option-click segment with scissors tool
- Ⓔ deleting a point deletes surrounding segments as well (opening closed paths)
- Ⓕ to move selection by distance specified in "Preferences" dialog box, press arrow key
- Ⓕ to layer objects, cut to clipboard, then choose "Paste in front" or "Paste in back" command to layer with respect to selected object
- Ⓕ to operate scale, flip, rotate, and skew tools, click near center of object to establish an origin, then drag to perform the transformation
- Ⓕ to display dialog and enter transformation specifications, option-click with transformation tool
- Ⓕ to transform and clone object simultaneously, press option before releasing with transformation tool
- Ⓕ create duplication series using "Transform again" command
- Ⓖ type may be transformed, filled, and stroked with any special line effect; type may also act as mask

Distinguishing features (cont.)

- ⊕ stroke options: caps, joins, and editable dash patterns
- ⊕ to create object-oriented patterns, layer rectangular tile boundary behind pattern objects and choose "Pattern"
- ⊕ transform tile patterns inside path or along with path
- ⊕ to determine placement of tile patterns, set ruler origin
- ⊕ to create a mask, layer the mask behind objects and combine mask and objects into single group
- ⊕ to create custom gradations, use blend tool
- ⊗ in preview mode, dithered screen colors accurately emulate Pantone colors on 8-bit color monitor
- ⊗ paths automatically break up if they are too complicated for limitations of specified printer
- ⊗ DrawOver utility converts PICT images into native PostScript files
- ⊗ Separator utility prints color separations

Deviations from the norm

- Ⓖ multiple type specs cannot be used in single text block
- Ⓖ text block limited to 255 characters
- Ⓖ text cannot be fit to a free-form path
- ⊕ arrow cap stroking option not available
- ⊗ imported MacPaint graphics will not print; use for tracing only
- ⊗ gray-scale or color scans cannot be imported or manipulated unless stored in EPS format
- ⊗ prints only to PostScript-equipped output devices, such as the LaserWriter Plus and NTX

Who needs Adobe Illustrator?

Illustrator lacks much of the structure associated with drawing programs. It provides no grids, and its "Alignment" command works on every point in a path, rather than aligning paths as a whole. The program is remarkably deficient in the area of text handling, but these problems are reported to be remedied in the next major upgrade (which may be available by time you read this). However, to th se who own PostScript printers and are interested primarily in free-form artwork, Illustrator's superb Bézier curve handling and high-end drawing features easily make up for its lack of structure. The program uses dithering to emulate the millions of colors that cannot be displayed with a standard 8-bit video card. It allows you to mask objects with type and to stroke type with any special line effect. All in all, it is arguably the finest drawing program available on the Macintosh.

Adobe Systems
1585 Charleston Rd.
Mountain View, CA
94039
(415) 961-4400

$495 retail
version reviewed: 1.9.3

Adobe Illustrator provides superb curve-handling features, making it possible to create any drawing you can imagine, regardless of complexity. If you use a PostScript printer, Illustrator is the best drawing program money can buy.

Aldus FreeHand

For the creation of free-form computer illustrations, the only serious competition to Adobe Illustrator is Aldus FreeHand, a program marketed and distributed by the same company that developed Page-Maker, the popular desktop publishing application. However, Free-Hand was created and continues to be upgraded by a small company called Altsys, whose other efforts include font-manipulation programs such as Fontographer, Art Importer, and Metamorphosis. In fact, Fontographer was the first Macintosh program to feature Bézier curve tools, well before their appearance in Adobe Illustrator. Its strengths over Illustrator include some of the best type control found in any application, including a command that converts type into paths that may be reshaped just as if they were drawn with the freehand tool; unlimited drawing layers, which allow you to create complex images modularly; a multiple undo/redo feature, supporting up to 100 consecutive undo commands; and a special image-editing feature for manipulating gray values of imported bitmaps.

Hardware requirements

- Macintosh Plus
- two Mbytes of RAM
- 20 Mbyte hard drive

Distinguishing features

- ❶ opens native, PICT, and Illustrator version 1.1 files
- ❶ imports MacPaint, TIFF, PICT, and EPS files
- ❶ saves in native format; exports in EPS Mac and PC formats
- ❷ geometric path tools: line, rectangle, rounded rectangle, and oval tools

Distinguishing features (cont.)

- **C** free-form path tools: freehand tool, corner, curve, and connector tools, and fully functioning Bézier curve tool (combination tool)

- **C** undraw mistakes with freehand tool by dragging with tool while pressing command key; draw straight segments by pressing option

- **D** marquee bitmap with trace tool to create many paths at a time

- **E** to select and reshape paths, use arrow tool; select path to displays points and Bézier control handles

- **E** to edit geometric shapes, first ungroup

- **E** to insert point into path, click segment with corner, curve, or connector tool

- **E** new segment automatically connects neighbors of deleted point, preventing break in outline of path

- **E** to display customized information dialog box and enter specifications, option-double-click any path or other object

- **F** deselect all paths by pressing tab; deselect points with ~ key

- **G** establish and manipulate multiple drawing layers using "Layers" palette

- **F** to transform selected object, drag with scale, flip, rotate, or skew tool

- **F** to display dialog and enter transformation specifications, option-click with transformation tool

- **F** information bar displays transformation particulars

- **F** repeat transformation with "Transform again" command; create duplication series using "Duplicate" command

- **G** comprehensive text formatting capabilities

- **G** fit text to free-form path using "Join" command

- **G** convert type set in any PostScript font into editable free-form paths with "Convert to paths" command

Distinguishing features (cont.)

- 🄗 stroke (line) options include caps, joins, and dash patterns; edit dash pattern by pressing option while selecting pattern
- 🄗 includes library of bitmapped fill patterns
- 🄗 to create object-oriented patterns, copy pattern objects to clipboard and choose "Tile"
- 🄗 transform tile patterns inside path or along with path
- 🄗 custom PostScript-language fill patterns available
- 🄗 to create a mask, cut objects to clipboard, select mask, and choose "Paste inside" command
- 🄗 automated gradation features include "Graduated" and "Radial"commands
- 🄗 to create custom gradations, use "Blend" command
- 🄧 imports and edits gray-scale and color scanned images
- 🄧 to scale bitmaps for optimal printing, option-drag corner handle

Deviations from the norm

- 🄐 native EPS files cannot be opened; you must save two versions of any file you intend to export
- 🄕 cannot select path in front of selected path unless you first deselect rear path by pressing tab
- 🄕 option-dragging an object does not create a clone; must choose "Clone" command, then drag clone to new location
- 🄗 filling and stroking features organized into complicated maze of commands and dialog boxes; many standard stroking and filling options cannot be applied to text
- 🄗 tiles in object-oriented pattern must be perfectly square
- 🄧 inadequate on-screen color display; relies exclusively on current system colors (no dithering)

Who needs Aldus FreeHand?

Much has been written about how FreeHand compares to Adobe Illustrator. But which one is truly better? In most respects, Illustrator is a better program for artists specifically interested in creating naturalistic artwork. Though FreeHand is also satisfactory for this purpose, Illustrator provides a more direct operating environment and fewer but more sophisticated drawing tools. If, however, you prefer a more structured environment involving grids, user-defined guidelines, and true alignment/distribution features, then FreeHand is the obvious choice. FreeHand also provides a powerful system of element information dialog boxes, which allow you to control the most minute details of your graphic, including the precise placement of Bézier control handles. FreeHand also provides some of the best bitmap handling of any software. Most of the figures in Chapter 9, for example, were created using FreeHand.

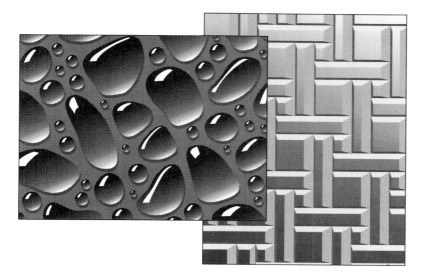

Aldus Corp.
411 First Ave. South
Seattle, WA
98104
(206) 622-5500

$495 retail
version reviewed: 3.0

These realistic, highly detailed images are typical of the kind of artwork you can produce using Aldus FreeHand. If you're interested in a structured, precise drawing environment, FreeHand is the program for you.

Canvas

Canvas is actually two programs. The first is a typical stand-alone application that you launch from the Finder and run by itself or in conjunction with other programs when using MultiFinder. The second, Canvas DA, is a desk accessory that allows you to open and edit object-oriented images while simultaneously using another piece of software, without the benefit of MultiFinder. Canvas DA must be installed into your System using the Font/DA Mover application or simply attached using a mounting utility such as Suitcase or Master-Juggler, after which it becomes accessible as a command under the Apple menu. (Under System 7.0, desk accessories will be handled differently.) Using Canvas DA, you don't have to exit a word processing or page-layout document to create graphics on-the-spot or make last-minute revisions to existing graphics. Both Canvas and Canvas DA combine moderate drawing and two-color painting capabilities, although the most advanced functions—layering, custom macro commands, and color palette modification—are missing from Canvas DA.

Hardware requirements

- Macintosh Plus
- at least one Mbyte of RAM (two Mbytes recommended)
- 20 Mbyte hard drive

Distinguishing features

- ⒶⒶ opens native, MacPaint, PICT, and TIFF files
- Ⓐ saves in native, MacPaint, PICT, and TIFF formats
- Ⓑ geometric path tools: line, arc, rectangle, rounded rectangle, and oval tools
- Ⓑ to edit the circumferance of an arc or the radius of rounded rectangle corners, drag circular handle

Distinguishing features (cont.)

C free-form path tools: freehand, polygon, Bézier curve tools

D to create many paths at a time, select bitmap and choose "Autotrace to" command

E to reshape, select free-form path and choose "Edit Pts" command from appropriate tool menu (or double-click path)

E to convert smooth point into corner point, press tab key and drag Bézier control handle

E to insert point into path, option-click segment in edit mode; delete point by shift-option-clicking

E new segment automatically connects neighbors of deleted point, preventing break in outline of path

E to display dialog box containing information about selected object, choose "Object" command

E to edit geometric shapes, choose "Object" and select a different icon from "Object type" pop-up menu

F to move selection one pixel, press arrow key; press command-arrow key to move selection 10 pixels; press option-arrow key to move selection 50 pixels

F to establish and manipulate multiple drawing layers, use "Layer manager" command

F scale object by dragging corner handle

F to flip, rotate, skew, distort, or apply perspective to selected object, use commands under the "Effects" menu

F information manager displays cursor coordinates

F to create duplication series, choose "Duplication" command and enter specifications in dialog box

G choose all text formatting commands from type tool menu; press shift to display type size menu, press option to display styles, press command to display fonts

Distinguishing features (cont.)

- **G** to check the spelling of selection or document, use "Spell check" commands
- **H** editable arrowhead cap options
- **D** to display dash patterns, option-click line manager icon
- **D** includes library of bitmapped fill patterns
- **X** to assign selected image as macro command, choose "Add macro" command
- **X** full bitmap painting and editing capabilities with up to 2540 dot-per-inch resolution
- **X** Canvas Separator utility prints color separations and converts drawings to EPS and Illustrator version 1.1 formats

Deviations from the norm

- **C** Bézier curve tool lacks certain functionalities; cannot constrain 45° segments, cannot draw a cusp (must draw smooth point and reshape)
- **D** cannot adjust sensitivity of freehand tool or "Autotrace to" command
- **E** points cannot be added to end of open path, nor can paths be split or joined
- **H** no cap or join stroking option, except arrowheads
- **H** strokes cannot be applied to text
- **H** no object-oriented tile-pattern capability
- **H** no masking, gradation, or blending capability
- **X** only black-and-white and two-color paintings can be edited

Who needs Canvas?

Generally, Canvas is a respectably strong program for combining colored objects and monochrome bitmaps in a single document. Object-oriented capabilities coexist in pleasant accord with sketching tools like the pencil, eraser, and paint can. You can define unlimited numbers of drawing layers for placing multiple images in front of and behind one another to easily produce complicated drawing structures. You may also define macro commands to repeat images you use on a regular basis. But in Canvas, the best features seem to be the simplest ones, such as the "Arrows" command, which allows you to manipulate the appearance of arrowhead line caps. The program is aimed at the low-end drawing market. It competes specifically with MacDraw and, in most ways, Canvas is the better program. Although its interface could use some refinement, Canvas offers substantially more features than MacDraw for about ¾ the price.

Deneba Software
3305 N.W. 74th Ave.
Miami, FL
33122
(305) 594-6965

$299.95 retail
version reviewed: 2.1

SALE PRICE: $29.95

Canvas provides an adept environment for combining bitmapped and object-oriented images into a single piece of artwork. Although its drawing tools don't hold a candle to those of Illustrator or FreeHand, it is a respectable, easy-to-use, medium-feature program.

MacDraw II

The prototypical and most popular drawing program on the Macintosh is MacDraw. To this day, MacDraw retains the fundamental strengths that made it an immediate success when Apple first introduced it over four years ago: its design is sleek and uncluttered, its tools are extremely easy to use, and the product as a whole is solidly consistent in performance. But alas, this reliable turtle of a program has allowed itself to fall far behind the rest of the object-oriented pack. In the hands of Claris, this established software offering has evolved more notably in the direction of word handling and slide presentation than in developing its overall graphic potential. MacDraw is still very useful for creating object-oriented images using readily identifiable tools and commands, but jackrabbits like Canvas and SuperPaint have long since outraced it in the medium-end features department. Slow and steady may win the race, but it's looking pretty grim here in the second round.

Hardware requirements

- Macintosh Plus
- one Mbyte of RAM
- dual 800K disk drives

Distinguishing features

- opens native and PICT files
- imports MacPaint images via the clipboard
- saves in native and PICT formats

Distinguishing features (cont.)

- **B** geometric path tools: line, arc, rectangle, rounded rectangle, and oval tools

- **B** to determine whether geometric shapes are drawn from corner or from center, toggle corner/center icon

- **C** free-form path tools: freehand and polygon tools

- **E** to reshape, select arc or free-form path and choose "Reshape" command

- **E** to insert point into path, click segment in reshape mode; delete point by option-clicking

- **E** new segment automatically connects neighbors of deleted point, preventing break in outline of path

- **E** to establish and manipulate multiple drawing layers, use "Layers" command; access layers by clicking up and down arrow icons

- **F** scale object by dragging corner handle

- **F** transformation commands: "Rotate," "Flip horizontal," and "Flip vertical"

- **F** to display transformation information, choose "Show size" command

- **F** to create duplication series, use "Duplicate" command

- **G** choose all text formatting commands from "Font," "Size," and "Style" menus

- **G** to check the spelling of selection or document, use "Spelling" commands

- **G** to notate parts of drawing, use stick-on labels created with note tool

Distinguishing features (cont.)

- ⓗ editable arrowhead cap options
- ⓗ to edit dash patterns, use "Dashes" command
- ⓗ includes library of bitmapped fill patterns
- ⓗ option-click bitmapped pattern to apply it to stroke of selected path
- ⓧ change layers to presentational slides by choosing "Turn slides on" command; access slides by clicking up and down arrow icons

Deviations from the norm

- ⓐ does not support EPS format
- ⓒ no Bézier curve tool nor any Bézier curve control
- ⓓ no tracing feature
- ⓔ points cannot be added to end of open path, nor can paths be split or joined
- ⓕ option-dragging an object does not create a clone; must use "Duplicate" command
- ⓕ limited transformation capabilities; no skewing
- ⓖ text cannot be scaled or flipped
- ⓗ no cap or join stroking option, except arrowheads
- ⓗ strokes cannot be applied to text
- ⓗ halftoned tints cannot be created; bitmapped patterns only
- ⓗ no object-oriented tile-pattern capability
- ⓗ no masking, gradation, or blending capability
- ⓧ eight colors only, regardless of video card capacity

Who needs MacDraw II?

For people who require a structured drawing environment, MacDraw has always been a dependable product, however rudimentary. MacDraw II builds on this tradition by adding surprisingly sophisticated ruler control. You may select from six pre-existing rulers or create and save your own. You may also specify your own drawing scales, so that an inch on your ruler might represent 3 ½ feet, eliminating the need for calculating the difference between an object in real life and its size in an architectural rendering or on a map. If you're looking for a introductory mix of CAD and presentational capabilities (with a spell-checker, no less) that doesn't require you to spend an inordinate amount of time fiddling with complex image-creation tools and commands, then MacDraw is probably your ideal program. But if you're on the prowl for naturalistic curves and refined PostScript drawing options, go back to Illustrator or FreeHand.

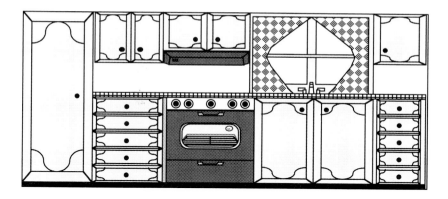

This image was created back in 1985 when MacDraw was brand new, but it could just as easily have been created yesterday. It displays all the classic earmarks of a piece of MacDraw artwork: bitmapped fill patterns, geometric shapes, and elementary curves, all stroked with a small collection of line weights. It isn't high art, but it's simple and it's adequate, just like MacDraw II.

Claris Corp.
440 Clyde Ave.
Mountain View, CA
94043
(408) 987-7000

$399 retail
version reviewed: 1.1

SuperPaint

When it was first released in late 1986, SuperPaint was the only graphics application to combine the bitmapping capabilities of MacPaint with the object-oriented precision of MacDraw. Since then, other programs, such as Canvas and UltraPaint, have followed suit. Although both of these programs surpass SuperPaint in one respect or another, SuperPaint still has a few bitmapping tricks up its sleeve. With the advent of "plug-ins," SuperPaint has broken fresh ground in the personal computer graphics arena. Possibly its strongest feature, plug-ins are tools that are created by third-party developers and may be added to SuperPaint's standard palette. SuperPaint comes with over 30 plug-in tools, all of which are applicable to the creation of bitmapped images only, but many of which are nonetheless impressive and utilitarian. You may alter the effects of these tools by double-clicking the tool icon, option-drawing with the tool, or applying other keyboard/mouse combinations. The sample image at the end of this section was created entirely with plug-in tools.

Hardware requirements

- Macintosh Plus
- at least one Mbyte of RAM
- dual 800K disk drives

Distinguishing features

- Ⓐ opens native, MacPaint, PICT, and Startup Screen files
- Ⓐ saves in native, MacPaint, PICT, and Startup Screen formats
- Ⓑ geometric path tools: line, arc, rectangle, rounded rectangle, and oval tools, as well as multigon tool for creating equilateral polygons with definable number of sides

Distinguishing features (cont.)

ⓒ free-form path tools: freehand and polygon tools

ⓓ to create many paths at a time, select bitmap and choose "Autotrace" command

ⓓ to adjust performance of tracing feature, use "Autotrace settings" command; to adjust freehand tool, use "Bézier settings" command

ⓔ to reshape, select arc or free-form path and choose "Reshape" command

ⓔ to toggle smooth point to corner point, double-click point

ⓔ to select multiple points in reshape mode, select one point and command-click others; to select range of points, select one point and shift-click another

ⓔ to insert point into path in reshape mode, option-click segment; delete point by pressing backspace or delete

ⓔ new segment automatically connects neighbors of deleted point, preventing break in outline of path

ⓔ to edit geometric shapes, use "Convert to Bézier" command

ⓕ to move selection one pixel, press arrow key

ⓕ to scale object, drag corner handle

ⓕ to scale, flip, rotate, skew, distort, or apply perspective to selected object or type, use commands under the "Transform" menu

ⓕ to display transformation information, choose "Show coordinates" command

ⓕ to create duplication series, use "Duplicate" command

ⓖ choose all text formatting commands from "Font" and "Text" menu

Distinguishing features (cont.)

- **H** editable arrowhead cap options
- **H** to edit dash pattern, use "Dashes" command
- **H** includes library of bitmapped fill patterns
- **H** full bitmap painting and editing capabilities with up to 2540 dot-per-inch resolution
- **X** over 30 plug-in tools; the effects may be modified by selecting line weights, pressing shift and option keys, double-clicking tool icons, and so on
- **X** plug-in commands include blend (bitmap only)

Deviations from the norm

- **A** does not support EPS format
- **C** no Bézier curve tool
- **E** points cannot be added to end of open path, nor can paths be joined
- **F** no cap or join stroking option, except arrowheads
- **H** neither strokes nor fills can be applied to text
- **H** halftoned tints cannot be created; bitmapped patterns only
- **H** no object-oriented tile-pattern capability
- **H** no masking or halftone-quality gradation or blending capabilities
- **X** only black-and-white and two-color paintings can be edited
- **X** eight colors only, regardless of video card capacity

Who needs SuperPaint?

SuperPaint's painting and drawing capabilities are assigned to two unique layers—a crude system compared with the infinite number of layers you may create in Canvas, any of which may contain both bitmaps and objects. This, plus the fact that SuperPaint is not available as a DA, has led many to surmise that Superpaint has become as much a has-been as MacDraw itself. However, SuperPaint offers a level of functionality that Canvas lacks. For example, SuperPaint offers the closest thing to real Bézier curve handling of any software short of Illustrator or FreeHand. Though it offers no point-by-point Bézier curve tool, you may edit any freehand image by moving points and adjusting Bézier control handles. And unlike Canvas, you may select multiple points, change the identity of a point from smooth to corner and back to smooth, split a path, and close or open a path. Also, you can adjust the sensitivity of both the freehand tool and the "Autotrace" command, a feature also missing from Canvas.

Silicon Beach Software

9770 Carroll Center
Rd., Suite J
San Diego, CA
92126
(619) 695-6956

$199 retail
version reviewed: 2.0

This bitmapped image was created entirely using SuperPaint's plug-in tools. For example, the central star was created with a single drag of the allGON tool, which allows you to specify virtually infinite shape-on-shape-on-shape patterns.

UltraPaint

UltraPaint is the only Macintosh program that combines object-oriented tools with full-color bitmap editing capabilities. The result is a unique image-processing application that is ideal for creating the kind of drawing/scanning hybrids we discussed in Chapter 9. Although UltraPaint provides no masking feature (so you cannot create figures like the last two in the previous chapter), it will allow you to edit the pixels in a scanned image, broadening your capabilities beyond the scope of our discussion. UltraPaint also provides a few full-fledged image-editing features. For example, you can sharpen the focus of an image or make it appear blurred. Using the special magic wand tool, you may select all pixels colored within a specified range. You may then apply commands to and even draw exactly inside the selected area. Previously found only in high-powered photo-editing software like Adobe Photoshop, the magic wand allows you to isolate images, altering only the foreground, the background, or some other detail in an image.

Hardware requirements

- Macintosh Plus
- two Mbyte of RAM
- 20 Mbyte hard drive

Distinguishing features

- **Ⓐ** opens native, MacPaint, PICT, TIFF, and Startup Screen files
- **Ⓐ** saves in native, MacPaint, PICT, TIFF, and Startup Screen formats
- **Ⓑ** geometric path tools: line, arc, rectangle, rounded rectangle, and oval tools

Distinguishing features (cont.)

- ⓑ to edit the circumferance of an arc or the radius of rounded rectangle corners, drag circular handle

- ⓒ free-form path tools: freehand, polygon, and Bézier curve tools

- ⓓ to create many paths at a time, select bitmap and choose "Autotrace to" command

- ⓓ to adjust performance of tracing feature, use "Autotrace options" command

- ⓔ to reshape, select free-form path and choose "Edit Pts" command from appropriate tool menu (or double-click path)

- ⓔ to convert smooth point into corner point, press tab key and drag Bézier control handle

- ⓔ to insert point into path, option-click segment in edit mode; delete point by shift-option-clicking

- ⓔ new segment automatically connects neighbors of deleted point, preventing break in outline of path

- ⓔ to display dialog box containing information about selected object, choose "Object" command

- ⓔ to edit geometric shapes, choose "Object" and select a different icon from the "Object type" pop-up menu

- ⓕ to move selection one pixel, press arrow key; to move selection 10 pixels, press command-arrow key; to move selection 50 pixels, press option-arrow key

- ⓕ to establish and manipulate multiple drawing layers, use "Layer manager" command

- ⓕ scale object by dragging corner handle

- ⓕ to flip, rotate, skew, distort, or apply perspective to selected object, use commands under the "Effects" menu

- ⓕ information manager displays cursor coordinates

Distinguishing features (cont.)

𝐅 to create duplication series, choose "Duplication" command and enter specifications in dialog box

𝐆 choose all text formatting commands from type tool menu; press shift to display type size menu, press option to display styles, press command to display fonts

𝐇 includes library of bitmapped fill patterns

𝐗 256-color bitmap painting and editing capabilities with up to 2540 dot-per-inch resolution

𝐗 external tools: magic wand, as well as many other color manipulation tools and commands

𝐗 commands at bottom of "Effects" menu produce photographic enhancements

𝐗 choose "Grayscale manager" command to adjust the brightness and contrast of a gray-scale scan

Deviations from the norm

𝐀 does not support EPS format

𝐂 Bézier curve tool lacks certain functionalities; cannot constrain 45° segment, cannot draw a cusp (must draw smooth point and reshape)

𝐃 sensitivity of freehand tool cannot be adjusted

𝐄 points cannot be added to end of open path, nor can paths be split or joined

𝐆 strokes cannot be applied to text

𝐇 no cap or join stroking options, except arrowheads

𝐇 arrowheads and dash patterns cannot be edited

𝐇 no object-oriented tile-pattern capability

𝐇 no object-oriented masking, halftone-quality gradation, or blending capabilities

Who needs UltraPaint?

Although UltraPaint's small collection of image-editing commands doesn't exactly rival those available in a dedicated color bitmap program, it does provide an excellent array of features, especially when you consider that it ties with SuperPaint for least expensive program reviewed in this chapter. However, despite its clever tools and sophisticated controls, UltraPaint suffers from printing oversights that limit its ultimate potential. First, the program provides no means for printing color separations. Second, because it provides no halftone control, you cannot print gray-scale images to a PostScript laser printer using Laser-Writer driver 5.2 or earlier. Typically, your best printing alternative is to save your artwork to disk and place it in a page-layout program—such as PageMaker or QuarkXPress—that will separate or halftone the image. UltraPaint's features make it an impressive first-version product. With some revisions, UltraPaint might become a real contender.

Deneba Software
3305 N.W. 74th Ave.
Miami, FL
33122
(305) 594-6965

$199 retail
version reviewed: 1.0

UltraPaint provides access to object-oriented and full-color bitmap editing tools under one roof. It even includes a handful of image-editing commands. Of these, we have applied the "Sharpen" command to focus the boxed area in this figure.

Appendices

Clip-Art Reference

Many graphics in this book are clip-art images. The following list itemizes the number of each page that contains a clip-art image, a description of the image, and the clip-art package from which the image originates. A second list includes specific vendor information for each clip-art package.

Note that most clip-art images in this book have been modified to some extent or another. Some of the clip-art is available only in a bitmapped format; it has been traced and refined in a drawing program for inclusion in this book. Do not expect a purchased clip-art image to exactly match one of our figures.

Pages that are not included in this listing contain original artwork created by the author.

Pages featuring clip-art images

PAGE	DESCRIPTION	PACKAGE NAME	PRODUCT LINE
7	headline fill pattern	Patterns & Textures	Collector's Edition
11	mortar board	Education 1	DeskTop Art
12	mortar board and car	Education 1	DeskTop Art
16	dog	Artfolio 1	DeskTop Art
17	ship	Seasonal 1	DeskTop Art/EPS
18	ship in bottle	Seasonal 1	DeskTop Art/EPS
20	Washington	Four Seasons 1	DeskTop Art
23	all Washingtons	Four Seasons 1	DeskTop Art
25	headline fill pattern	Patterns & Textures	Collector's Edition
27	cat (form icon)	Artfolio 1	DeskTop Art
30	dolls	Artfolio 1	DeskTop Art
32	Mona Lisa	Potpourri 1	DeskTop Art/EPS
34	lower bird	Graphics & Symbols 1	DeskTop Art
36	cat	Artfolio 1	DeskTop Art
39	right fish	Graphics & Symbols 1	DeskTop Art
41	lions	Accents & Borders 1	Images with Impact!
43	football players	Sports 1	DeskTop Art
46	eagle and killer whale	Graphics & Symbols 1	Images with Impact!
47	bowler	Athletics 1	DeskTop Art/EPS
48	bowler	Athletics 1	DeskTop Art/EPS
50	United States	USA	MacAtlas/Atlas PC
52	man at bottom of cliff	Business Images 2	Cliptures
52	car on top of cliff	EPS Business Art	ClickArt
56	left elephant	Artfolio 1	DeskTop Art
57	right fish	Sports 1	DeskTop Art
63	space shuttle	Business Images 2	Cliptures
85	headline fill pattern	Patterns & Textures	Collector's Edition
100	fish	Athletics 1	DeskTop Art/EPS
101	painters	Graphics & Symbols 1	DeskTop Art
102	painters	Graphics & Symbols 1	DeskTop Art
114	hamburger	EPS Illustrations	ClickArt
116	chalk and slate	Accents & Borders 1	Images with Impact!

PAGE	DESCRIPTION	PACKAGE NAME	PRODUCT LINE
119	hands	Business Images 2	Cliptures
120	hands	Business Images 2	Cliptures
121	hands	Business Images 2	Cliptures
122	hands	Business Images 2	Cliptures
144	tile pattern	Patterns & Textures	Collector's Edition
145	fish	Graphics & Symbols 1	DeskTop Art
149	headline fill pattern	Patterns & Textures	Collector's Edition
166	hockey player	Athletics 1	DeskTop Art/EPS
169	hockey player	Athletics 1	DeskTop Art/EPS
170	hockey player	Athletics 1	DeskTop Art/EPS
195	headline fill pattern	Patterns & Textures	Collector's Edition
198	page ornaments	Business Image	ClickArt
210	left cartoon	Business & Finance	Presentation Task Force
210	center cartoon	Volume 13	Digit-Art
210	right cartoon	Leisure Time 1	DeskTop Art/EPS
231	headline fill pattern	Patterns & Textures	Collector's Edition
234	left silhouette	Business Images 2	Cliptures
234	next-to-left silhouette	Seasonal 1	DeskTop Art/EPS
234	next-to-right silhouette	Business Images 2	Cliptures
234	right silhouette	Design Elements 1	DeskTop Art/EPS
253	logo elements	Graphics & Symbols 1	Images with Impact!
261	headline fill pattern	Patterns & Textures	Collector's Edition
264	young man	Business 1	Images with Impact!
264	stapler	Business Art	ClickArt
264	misty forest	Natural Images 1	Artbeats
274	sun	Accents & Borders	Images with Impact!
275	sun	Accents & Borders	Images with Impact!
283	headline fill pattern	Patterns & Textures	Collector's Edition
284	owls	School Days 1	DeskTop Art/EPS
286	owls	School Days 1	DeskTop Art/EPS
287	clown and dog	Seasonal 1	DeskTop Art/EPS
288	clowns	Seasonal 1	DeskTop Art/EPS

PAGE	DESCRIPTION	PACKAGE NAME	PRODUCT LINE
289	clowns	Seasonal 1	DeskTop Art/EPS
291	musical instruments	Accents & Borders	Images with Impact!
292	cartoon man	Business Images 1	Cliptures
292	sitting woman	Business Images 2	Cliptures
292	standing woman	Business Images 2	Cliptures
293	hand	Potpourri 1	DeskTop Art/EPS
293	naturalistic scissors	Potpourri 1	DeskTop Art/EPS
294	woman	Potpourri 1	DeskTop Art/EPS
294	leaning man	Business Images 2	Cliptures
294	girl with flowers	Seasonal 1	DeskTop Art/EPS
295	bunnies and bird	Seasonal 1	DeskTop Art/EPS
296	bunnies and bird	Seasonal 1	DeskTop Art/EPS
299	dancing woman	Art Nouveau Images	Masterworks
300	city images	Graphics & Symbols	Images with Impact!
301	city scene	Graphics & Symbols	Images with Impact!
302	left border	EPS Business Art	ClickArt
302	bamboo border	Accents & Borders	Images with Impact!
302	right border	Potpourri 1	DeskTop Art/EPS
303	rockin' dude	Leisure Time 1	DeskTop Art/EPS
303	heavy border	Accents & Borders	Images with Impact!
304	rockin' dude	Leisure Time 1	DeskTop Art/EPS
304	light border	Accents & Borders	Images with Impact!
305	rockin' dude	Leisure Time 1	DeskTop Art/EPS
305	medium-weight border	Accents & Borders	Images with Impact!
307	headline fill pattern	Patterns & Textures	Collector's Edition
313	woman	Business 1	Images with Impact!
313	fan motifs	Accents & Borders	Images with Impact!
315	woman's head	Seasonal 1	DeskTop Art/EPS
321	headline fill pattern	Patterns & Textures	Collector's Edition
327	Mac II with globe	EPS Business Art	ClickArt
331	water droplets	Natural Images 1	Artbeats
331	beveled texture	Dimensions 1	Artbeats

Vendor information

ArtBeats
Artbeats
PO Box 20083
San Bernandino, CA 92406
compatible with both Macs and PCs
(714) 881-1200

ClickArt
T/ Maker Company
1973 Landings Dr.
Mountain View, CA 94043
compatible with both Macs and PCs
(415) 962-0195

Cliptures
Dream Maker Software
7217 Foothill Blvd.
Tujunga, CA 91042
compatible with both Macs and PCs
(818) 353-2297

Collector's Edition
Adobe Systems Inc.
1585 Charleston Rd.
Mountain View, CA 94039
compatible with Macs only
(415) 961-4400

DeskTop Art (bitmapped)
DeskTop Art/EPS
Dynamic Graphics, Inc.
6000 N. Forest Park Dr.
Peoria, IL 61614
compatible with both Macs and PCs
(800) 255-8800

Digit-Art
Image Club Graphics, Inc.
1902 Eleventh St., SE
Calgary, Alberta, Canada T2G 3G2
compatible with both Macs and PCs
(403) 262-8008

Images with Impact!
3G Graphics
11410 NE 124th St., Suite 6155
Kirkland, WA 98034
compatible with both Macs and PCs
(206) 823-8198

MacAtlas
Atlas PC
MicroMaps
PO Box 757
Lambertville, NJ 08530
compatible with both Macs and PCs
(609) 397-1611

Masterworks
Silicon Designs
PO Box 2234
Orinda, CA 94563
compatible with Macs only
(415) 254-1460

Presentation Task Force
New Vision Technologies, Inc.
Box 5468, Station F
Ottawa, Ontario, Canada K2C 3M1
compatible with PCs only
(613) 727-8184

Index

PostScript language   186, 188
    laser printers   326
"Preferences" command   211, 247, 325
presentation   26, 28–36
    guidelines   33–35
"Preview" command   196
primary colors   78
printers   80
    laser   186
        PostScript   326
printing   79–81
    commercial   80
    process color   80
    spot color   80
process color printing   80
proportion   26, 53–59
    exaggerated   56–58
    recording accurately   55–56
    similarizing   58–59
    uses for   55
proximity   47

Q

QuarkXPress   347

R

radial gradations   145
"Radial"command   330
raised type   176
realistic graphic   263
    clip-art   292
    examples of   264
    guidelines   263
rectangle tool   74, 88, 90
red light   78
reference lines   274
reference points   60
reflected light   76–77, 278
"Reshape" command   104, 337, 341
reshape tool   103
reshaping
    free-form paths   104–105
    geometric paths   105–107
    paths   103–112
    rounded rectangles   106

resolution   186
reusing a graphic   17
"Rotate" command   120, 337
rotating   120
rotation tool   120, 325, 329
round cap   138
"Round Corners" command   106
round join   137
rounded rectangle tool   88, 90
rulers   87

S

saving a drawing   17–18
scale   26, 45–53
    recording accurately   45–46
    uses for   45
scale tool   118, 325, 329
scaling   118–119
    to indicate distance   47–49
    for drama   51–53
    to indicate importance   49–51
scanners   308–309
scans   307
    backgrounds   312–314
    examples of   309
    importing into FreeHand   330
    importing into Illustrator   326
    masking   315–316
    tile patterns   314–315
    transforming   310–312
scissors tool   216
    adding point with   325
screen frequency   186
scroll bars   87
SE   77
segments   93
    adjusting curvature   108–109
    deleting   216
selecting
    multiple paths   113
    multiple points   107
    paths   113
    points   107
    type   126
"Send to back" command   115
sensitivity options   247

This title is also available in a special PC edition.

Includes information about Corel® Draw, Micrografx® Designer™, Arts & Letters®, Adobe Illustrator®, and GEM® Artline™

Also available from
BUSINESS ONE IRWIN

Mastering Aldus® FreeHand™
Deke McClelland & Craig Danuloff
ISBN 1-55623-288-8   Order #32888

Mastering Adobe® Illustrator 88™
Deke McClelland & Craig Danuloff
ISBN 1-55623-157-1   Order #31571

Painting on the Macintosh®
Deke McClelland
ISBN 1-55623-265-9   Order #32659

The PageMaker® Companion Macintosh Version 4.0
Craig Danuloff & Deke McClelland
ISBN 1-55623-355-8   Order #33558

*Purchase these titles at your local bookseller
or call BUSINESS ONE IRWIN*